ROBERT WAYNE DUNCAN · DANIELLE DUNN · GARY W. DUNN · LIZETE DUREAULT · JOHN H.G. DUSTAN · ANTHONY DUTTON · MARISE DUTTON · PETER R.

THOMAS S. DYBHAVN · HENRY I. DYE · ROBERT E. EADES · MALCOLM E.S. EARLE · WM. D.S. EARLE · R. HENRY EASINGWOOD · JAMES

CHRISTIAN EBBEHOJ · BRIAN D. EDGAR · JUDITH EDGAR · L. BRUCE EDMOND · THOMAS EDSTRAND · IAN EDWARDS · T. BENTLEY EDWA

WALTER EGGLETON · AMY EGGLETON-DUNBAR · JULIA EHMAN · INES EISSES · JOHN A. EKELS · HUGH S. ELAND · REG ELAND · J.S. ELLETT · DOUG

BARNEY ELLIS-PERRY · ROGER DUNCAN ELMES · STEFEN JAMES ELMITT · PETER ELMS · JACK C. ELSEY · FLEMMING ELVIN-JENSEN · JUSTIN EL

JAN EMERTON · WM. R. EMERTON · MARK C. ENDERSBY · KRISTA ENGELLAND · ROBERT P. ENGLE · GORDON G. ENGLISH · MARTIN

JOHN H. EVANS · P.V.O. EVANS · R.N.P. EVANS · SHERRY LYNN EVANS · A. WILLIAM EVERETT · DAVID R. EVERETT · JEFF EVERETT · PETER D. E

ROSS HARRISON FAHRNI · IAN FALCONER · WILLIAM VINCENT FALCUS · ISABELLE FALKINS · PETER MORGAN FARGEY · CHRISTOPHER FARNWORTH · J. RAMSAY M. FARRAN · NANCY FARRAN

DIANE K. FAST · MALCOLM FAVIELL · MARC FELLIS · MAURICE FELLIS · DAVID E. FENN · MICHAEL D. FENN · EUGENE FENTON · KEN FERCHOFF · COLLIN FERGUSON · NIGEL FERGUSON

WILLIAM J. FERGUSON JR. · ED A. FERREIRA · C.C. JOCK FERRIE · GILLIAN FEYER · H. FREDERICK FIELD · KENNETH M. FIELD · KELLY FIELDER · CATHERINE FIELD-JAGGER

GRENVILLE P. FINCH-NOYES · MATTHEW FINCH-NOYES · ROBERT FINDLAY · ANDRA FINLAY · DAVID K. FINLAY · MARK FINLAY · EILEEN FINNEGAN · WILLIAM FITZGERALD · GORDON E. FLACK

GREGOR C.H. FLECK · BALT R. FLEISCHER · PAUL FLESHER · BRADLEY L. FLETCHER · DAVID FLETCHER · BRIAN FOLEY · CLINTON W. FOOTE · DOUGLAS FORD · KAREN FORD · PERRY B. FORD

ROBERT A. FORREST · BRIAN FORST · VERNON FORSTER · A.J.B. FORSYTH · BENJAMIN A.C. FORSYTH · BRETT J. FORSYTH · ROBERT FORSYTH · VIRGINIA FORSYTH · WM. M. FORSYTH

REX E. FORTESCUE · RICHARD E. FORTESCUE · DEBORAH FORTESCUE-MERRIN · COLIN E. FOSTER · LORING W. FOSTER · JOAN FOSTER-KLINE · LARRY J. FOURNIER · BRENT C. FRANCIS

HELEN ANNE FRANKLIN · BRUCE F. FRASER · DAVID K. FRASER · DOUGLAS FRASER · GRAHAM FRASER · IAN FRASER · RANALD CRAIG FRASER · REAR ADMIRAL JAMES D. FRASER · ROBERT M. FRASER

RUSSELL B. FRASER · RUSSELL G. FRASER · IAN D. FREEMAN · PATRICIA FREEMAN · SYDNEY M. FRIEDMAN · DAVID E. FRISBY · LAWRENCE FRONCZEK · BARRY ROBERT FULFORD

JENNIFER GABLE · MARIANNE GADBAN · SIMON GADBAN · PATTI A. GAINER · MICHAEL GALAMBOS · CLARK V. GALLON · BRIAN J. GARDENER-EVANS · MARGARET GARDINER · PAMELA GARDNER

ROBERT C. GARDNER · DONALD G. GARNETT · ADRIAN JAMES GATRILL · P. NICHOLAS GEER · MICHAEL GEIST · PETER D. GELPKE · WALTER GFELLER · TREVOR J. GIBBONS · PETER GIBBS

COLIN J. GIBSON · GORDON GIBSON · JENNIFER GIBSON · MARC GIBSON · NANCY ANN GIBSON · ROBERT GIBSON · ROBERT GIBSON JR. · THILO GIESE · MAUREEN GILL · PAUL GILL

BRIAN GILLEY · HELEN GILLEY · JASON C. GILLEY · BETH GILLIES · DOUGLAS M. GILLILAND · JOHN M. GILLIS · PETER R. GIRLING · GRAEME C. GISH · JOHN O. GJERVAN · JAMES P. GLADSTONE

JAMES GLASS · ROBERT K. GLASS · J. ROGER GLASSFORD · GORDON H. GLOSTER · ARTHUR D. GOBIN · ASHLEY GOLDBERG · MURRAY GOLDBERG · D.M.M. GOLDIE · ALLAN GOLDSMITH

LARRY M. GOLDSTEIN · KELLY-ANN GOOD · GEOFFREY N. GOODALL · ROGER GOODALL · F. DAVID GOODING · LISA GOODING · DAVID GOODMAN · JONI GOODMAN · MILTON J. GOODMAN

GRANTE GOODWYN · HAROLD W. GOODWYN · BRUCE MACMILLAN GORDON · C.H. JOHN GORDON · HAROLD GORDON · HUNTLY GORDON · TIMOTHY R. GOULD · WM. P. GOULD

D. HENRY GOURLAY · CATHERINE GOURLEY · JEFFREY D. GOW · DAVID E. GRAHAM · DONALD J. GRAHAM · J. ANDREW GRAHAM · JAMES S. GRAHAM · JAMIE GRAHAM · JOHN A. GRAHAM

LOUISE GRAHAM · PHILIP GRAHAM · MICHAEL GRAHAME · SCOTT GRANGER · GORDON CHARLES GREEN · R. ADAIR GREEN · BRUCE M. GREGG · GERHARD GRIEP · WILLIAM R. GRIERSON

THOMAS F.A. GRIFFIN · DERYL R. GRIFFITH · KEN R. GRIFFITH · VIKKI LAUREEN GRIFFITH · EMILY GRIFFITHS · JEFFREY GRIFFITHS · DARYL A. GRIMSON · J.G. GRIMSTON · LOUISE GRIMWOOD

ROBERT GRITTEN · LARRY B. GROBERMAN · AVRIL GROVE · PETER F. GROVE · BERNARD GUAY · STEIN K. GUDMUNDSETH · CONRAD B. GUELKE · KAREN GUELKE · JANINE GUENTHER

GAYLE GUEST · GOWAN T. GUEST · WAYNE F. GUINN · TRAUDI GULD · GREGORY A. GUREL · JOHN B. HAGUE · JOSEPH MARTIN HALEY · DOUGLAS J. HALL · JOHN B. HALL · KENNETH L. HALL

SCOTT B. HALL · DERMOT C. HALLARAN · GRAHAM HALLAT · KENNETH HALLAT · SVEN HALLE · RICHARD SULLIVAN HALLISEY · ROBERT HALPENNY · JOHN HALSE · ALISON HAMILTON

ANDREW HAMILTON · MARGARET HAMILTON · PATRICIA HAMILTON · GRANT C. HANKIN · JERRY HANLON · MARK HANNA · ALAN G. HANNAM · COLIN G. HANSEN · COLBY HARDER

C. WILLIAM HARDY · GERALD HARDY · MICHAEL HARDY · PHILIP HARLAND · JENNIFER HARMAN · R. GREG HARMS · JANE HARPER · HARLEY HARRIS · RICHARD A. HARRIS · ROBERT J. HARRIS

ALEX R. HARRISON · HORACE W.R. HARRISON · DAVID A. HARSTONE · MARY HARTNELL · WAYNE HARTRICK · ALLAN J. HARVEY · ERIC R.O. HARVEY · BRIAN HARWOOD · DAVID HASLAM

RAY B. HASLAM · RICHARD F. HATCH · PETER HATFIELD · LESLIE HAUSCH · ROBERT N. HAUSCH · CHANTAL HAUSSMANN · IRVIN FRANCIS HAWORTH · CHRISTINE HAY · JENNIFER HAYES

JOHN HAYLEY · JOHN G.A. HAZELDINE · SCOTT B. HEAN · DAVID G. HEANEY · JAMES C. HEANEY · ROY H.G. HEARN · SANDRA LYNN HEATH · ELIZABETH HEDGES · GEORGE HEDGES

JAMES W. HEINMILLER · EBERHARD HEINZEMANN · MERVYN HEMPENSTALL · RICHARD HEMSWORTH · BYRON HENDER · DOUGLAS HENDERSON · GORDON HENDERSON

PAUL HENDERSON · PETER HENDRIE · JANE HENLEY · MATTHEW HENLEY · RORY HENRY · RONALD HEPTING · MARC HERRMANN · TERRY G. HESELTON · ALAN HETHERINGTON · RUTH HEYES

SUSAN HEYES · CHRISTINE E. HIBBARD · SCOTT GREGORY HICKS · WALTER A. HICKS · TONY HIEDA · DAVID HIGGS · MICHAEL L. HIGGS · UWE W. HILDEBRANDT · BRIAN J.B. HILL

DIANA R. HILL · JEREMY M. HILL · PATRICK N. HILL · ROBERT H. HILL · ROSS K. HILL · WILLIAM M. HILL · TINA HILLS · JOHN A. HILTON · MARK W. HILTON · TERRY HIND · DENNIS HNATYSZEN

DAVID T.K. HO · DON G. HOBBS · CARAGH HODGE · ALEXANDER HOELK · CLAUS HOELK · FRIEDRICH HOELK · G. NEIL HOKONSON · SALLY HOLDEN · CHARLES W. HOLDER

FIRE CHIEF RAY HOLDGATE · ROBERT W. HOLE JR. · ADRIENNA HOLLAND · MELISSA M. HOLLAND · PHYLLIS D. HOLLAND · TERRY HOLLAND · MONIKA HOLM-BERGINS · DOUGLAS K. HOLME

CHERYL HOLMES · MARY HOLMES · DOUGLAS HOLTBY · LARISSA IRENE HOOLEY · JEREMY H.V. HOOPER · SUSAN HOOPER · FABIAN JOHN S. HOPE · TIMOTHY HOPKINS · JUDITH HORNE

LYNN HORTON · LIONEL HOULE · WILLIAM L. HOURSTON · PETER HOUSE · GORDON HOUSTON · BRENT I. HOWARD · GREGORY C. HOWARD · HELEN HOWARD · IAN HOWARD

JOHN HOWARD · SARAH HOWARD · DOUGLAS HOWDEN · CATHERINE HOWELL · JEFFREY HOWEY · DAVID A. HUGHES · SANDRA HUGHES · TANYA HUGHES · TIMOTHY HUGHES · TOM HUGHES

WILLIAM C. HUGHES · TERENCE CHI-YAN HUI · TREVOR W. HULL · RICK W. HULLAH · BARRY J. HUME · BENJAMIN L. HUME · CHARLIE HUME · EDWARD J. HUME · GAVIN ALEXANDER HUME

STEPHANIE HUME · ROBERT H. HUNCHAK · RODERICK M. HUNGERFORD · BRENT EDWARD HUNTER · BRIAN T. HUSE · DAN HUSTY · KEATH HUTTON · BASIL C. HUXHAM · JEAN HYATT

E. KELLY HYSLOP · JAMES HYSLOP · PETER J. HYSLOP · JANET INGLEDEW · TODD INGLEDEW · GLENN A. IRVING · JOHN IRVING · VICTOR IRVING · JOHN J. IRWIN · RICHARD T. IRWIN

DEAN J ISAAC · MARK F. ISAAK · KENNETH G. ISARD · BARCLAY ISHERWOOD · COLIN JACKSON · DAVID JACKSON · PER JACOBSEN · CAROLINE JAMES · MICHELLE DIANE JAMES · SANDRA JAMES

ROBERT A. JAMIESON · PATRICIA JANZEN · GEOFFREY JARMAN · JOHN JARMAN · PAUL L. JARRETT · GEOFFREY JARVIS · LOTHAR JASCHKE · DWIGHT A. JEFFERSON · FRASER JEFFERSON

PETER N. JEFFERSON · BRUCE E. JEFFERYS · DAVID E. JEFFERYS · E.E. TED JEFFERYS · JOHN P. JENKINS · RICHARD F. JENKINS · TREVOR W. JENKINS · COLIN N. JENKINSON · DAVIDSON JENNINGS

KENNETH JENS · J. MICHAEL JENSEN · JACK JERVIS · LUCILLE M.B. JERVIS · MICHAEL J. JERVIS · GARY H. JOHNCOX · CATHERINE JOHNSON · KRISTOFOR L. JOHNSON · L. BRETT JOHNSON

LYNN JOHNSON · MARY ALICE JOHNSON · WILLIAM A. JOHNSON · CHRISTOPHER M. JOHNSTON · D. LUKIN JOHNSTON · DAVID M. JOHNSTON · GREGORY JOHNSTON · JAMES JOHNSTON

LYLE W. JOHNSTON · W. MURRAY JOHNSTON · F.R.C. JOHNSTONE · IAIN R.C. JOHNSTONE · DARRELL D. JONES · JEREMY A. JONES · KEITH M. JONES · MICHAEL W. JONES · RANDALL H. JONES

RUSSELL A.E. JONES · T.V. JONES · VICTOR JONES · DAVID S. JORDAN · RALPH D. JORDAN · ANDREW JORDAN-KNOX · FINN JORGENSEN · BRITTA JOYCE · NIKOLAS JOYCE · PAUL D. JOYCE

ALEXANDER DAVID JUKES · CAROL JUKES · CHRISTOPHER JUKES · RONALD JUPP · VLADIMIR KAHLE · EDGAR F KAISER JR. · ANITA KALYANPUR · DONALD J. KAVANAGH · PETER B.L. KEATE

JANE KEAY · BRIAN DOUGLAS KEIR · MORAY KEITH · JOHN KEITH-KING · JONATHAN KEITH-KING · ANDREW KEMP · DUDLEY KENDALL · WILLIAM D. KENDRICK · DAVID S. KENNEDY

DOUGLAS SCOTT KENNEDY · JONATHON KENNEDY · A.M.C. KENNING · CARL W. KENNING · BRENTON D. KENNY · ROBERT KENNY · RUSSELL A. KER · MICHAEL KERFOOT · RUDY KERKLAAN

DARCY R. KERNAGHAN · JAMES R. KERR · KELLY ANNE KERR · LYDA KERR · LYLE H. KERR · W. BRENT KERR · H.F. KERRIN · JAMES W.P. KERSHAW · WILLIAM H. KERSHAW

CHAPIN KEY · SUSAN KEY · BEHZAD KHOSROWSHAHI · ELIZABETH KIDD · JOANIE KIDNER · WILLIAM E. KIDNER · WILLIAM T. KIDNER · CARLYLE KILLAM · EUGENE KILLAM · F. WM. KILLAM

F.R. (BILL) KILLAM · G. JAMES KILLAM · HAYDEN HOOD KILLAM · KARA KILLAM · KYLY KILLAM · MICHAEL KILLAM · PETER H. KILLAM · PAUL KILLEEN · FRANK KILLORAN · JOHN KINE

JOHN ROBERT M. KING · R. MILES KINGAN · ERNEST J. KINGSLEY · HUGH A.G. KINGSMILL · JOHN T. KINNEY · STEVE KINSEY · WILLIAM D. KINSEY · MATTHEW ROBERT KIRK-BUSS

CAROLYN KIRKLAND · KENNETH P. KIRKLAND · TROY KIRTZ · SHERRY KLIMEK · JOHN KLYMAK · GREG KNIGHT · RUPERT J. KNIGHT · STEPHEN A. KNIGHT · LT. COL. A.A. KNIGHT RETD.

LYALL D. KNOTT · DEREK W. KNOX · JOHN MICHAEL ANTHONY KOERNER · JASON PATRICK KOSHMAN · JOHN S. KOWALCHUK · LORNE T. KRAMER · DEANNA KRATZENBERG · TREVOR KRAY

5

Racers and Rovers

JAMES P. DELGADO

FOREWORD BY PETER C. NEWMAN

Racers and Rovers

100 Years of the Royal Vancouver Yacht Club

DOUGLAS & McINTYRE

VANCOUVER/TORONTO

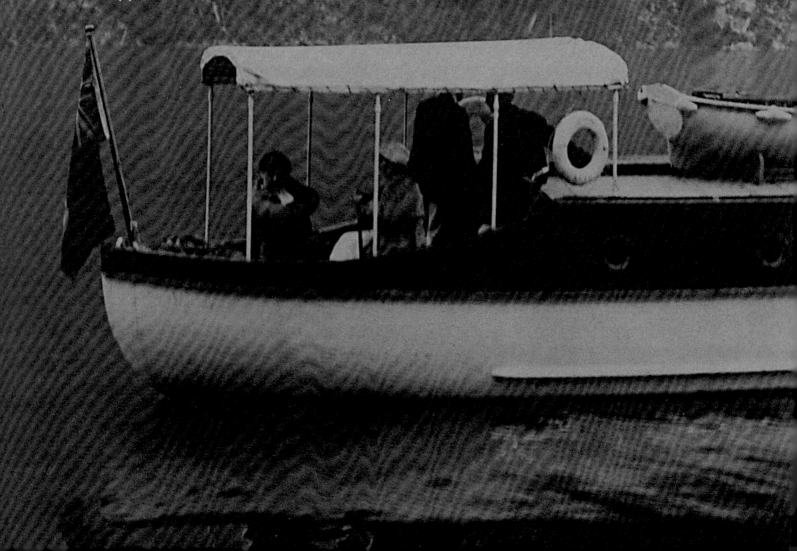

Douglas & McIntyre
2323 Quebec Street, Suite 201
Vancouver, British Columbia v5t 4s7
www.douglas-mcintyre.com

National Library of Canada Cataloguing in Publication Data
Delgado, James P.
Racers and rovers : 100 years of the Royal Vancouver Yacht Club /
James P. Delgado.
Includes bibliographical references and index.
ISBN 1-55054-988-x
1. Royal Vancouver Yacht Club–History. 2. Yachting–British
Columbia–Vancouver–History. I. Title.
GV823.R68D44 2003   797.1'246'06071133   C2003-910518-0

Editing by Saeko Usukawa
Design by George Vaitkunas
Printed and bound in Canada by Friesens
Printed on acid-free paper

The publisher gratefully acknowledges the financial support of the
Canada Council for the Arts, the British Columbia Arts Council,
and the Government of Canada through the Book Publishing
Industry Development Program (BPIDP) for its publishing activities.

All photographs are from the collection of the Royal Vancouver
Yacht Club, unless otherwise credited in the captions.

Every effort has been made to trace ownership of the photographs
in this book. Errors or omissions will be corrected in future edi-
tions, provided notification is sent to the publisher.

Front endpaper photo: Four Ed Monk-designed sister boats on sea
trials in Vancouver Harbour, 1961.
Back endpaper photo: A "spinnaker parade" of boats. James
McVie photo, RVYC
Frontispiece: The traditions of Opening Day go back to the origins
of yachting and draw heavily on naval tradition. Painting by Bill
Beadle, RVYC Collection
Pages iv and v photo: The Akhurst family aboard their 37-foot
I'llaway, built in 1911.
Pages vi and vii photo: The Jericho mooring basin.
Page viii photo: *Spirit*, n.d.
Page xi photo: Club members enjoying a powerboat cruise in the
1930s.
Page xii photo: Star Class boats *Astrea* (in the lead) and *Auriga*
racing on the waters of English Bay, circa 1923.

CONTENTS

A hundred years is a measure of time, but when an organisation has kept going successfully for that time, it becomes a major achievement and a matter of pride for all its members. I am delighted to have this opportunity to congratulate all the members of the Royal Vancouver Yacht Club on the achievement of its centennial. I feel that I have been associated with the Club for half that period, as I presented The Duke of Edinburgh's Trophy for the Dragon Class, when I paid a visit to the Club back in 1953. I then became even more closely associated with it by becoming Patron in 1976.

I think that all the members can feel well satisfied with a club that has done so much for yachting on the West Coast. The very high reputation of the Club, both nationally and internationally, reflects the commitment and dedication of all its Commodores, Flag Officers and Committee Members throughout its existence and I have no doubt this will continue long into the future.

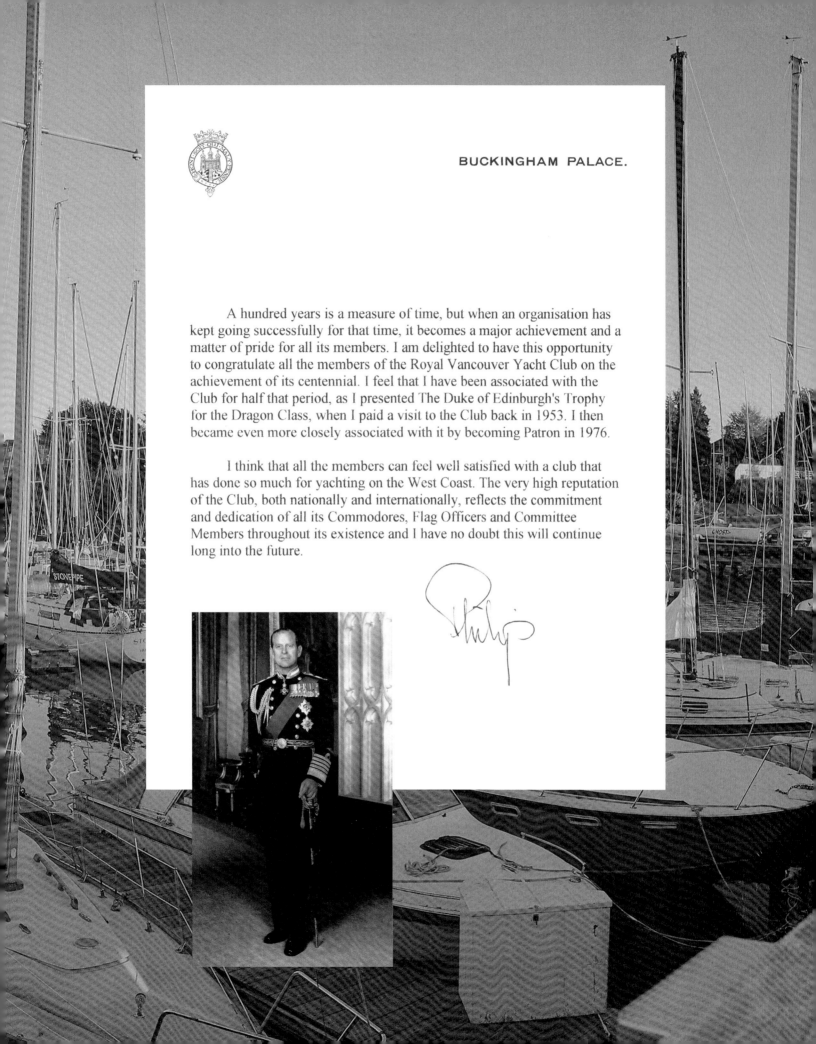

Centennial Book Patrons

James P. Angus

Roy & Sheila Appleford

Underhill/Bickerstaff Family

Bill Botham & Family

Jim Case & Family

Tom & Maggi Christy

Ronald and Ardelle Cliff

Bob Conconi & Family

Paul Cosulich & Family

George & Janet Cunningham

Douglas R. Day & Family

John Dew & Family

John Downie & Family

Ken & Mary Downie

Everett Family

A.J.B. Forsyth

Robert Gibson

Bruce M. Gordon

David Jordan

Ralph Jordan

Mary Jane & Allan Laird

Philip Langridge & Family

Shane & Jaana Lunny

Iain Mackay

John MacPhail & Family

Don & Annabelle Martin

Bob Matthews & Family

Wayne Naylor & Family

John & Lynne Newton

Bob Nowack & Family

Brian O'Sullivan & Family

Robert L. & Robert G. Payne

Heinz Rautenberg & Family

David & Margaret Rolfe

R. Bruce Russell

Dave Russell & Family

Marc Sandercombe & Family

Richard & Nancy Self

Anthony Sessions

Dan Sinclair & Family

Alan & Thomas Skidmore

David & Gaylean Sutcliffe

Bob & Heather Thomson

Mark Webber

Jordan & Louise Welsh

J. Alex Wood & Family

Bernice Bell:
In Memory of Harry Elliot Bell

James Dudley:
In Memory of Jean Almas

Jean Meakin & Family:
In Memory of Arthur Meakin

Mrs. Joyce MacCrostie-Shives:
In Memory of Dr. Watson MacCrostie

Randy Olafson:
In Memory of Mr. Robert Butt

Ken Rooney & Family:
In Memory of Doan Hartnell

FOREWORD

CHRONICLING THE HISTORY of any institution is an essential exercise in defining and perpetuating its existence. Its future is purchased by its past. This evocative book captures the first century of the Royal Vancouver Yacht Club's story, eloquently and elegantly, in the wide sweeps that readable, image-oriented history demands. The club executives chose wisely and well. Author James Delgado captures the essence not just of the events that transpired but of the history that those events added up to. *Racers and Rovers* rings true as a permanent record of the wonderful foibles, loyal comradeship and unquenchable spirit that has characterized the Royal Vancouver Yacht Club.

Delgado, who is a born storyteller with a pronounced maritime bent, manages to catch the great unspoken nuance that has motivated every member since the club began, in 1903: namely, that owning a boat seldom qualifies as a rational act. Instead, it plays to the romantic side in all of us. It's that element that makes our club time so magical. What brings us together is the realization that there is nothing on God's Earth that equals the pleasures of boating on Canada's west coast. Nothing. Those precious and all too brief summer days we spend on the water affirm Joseph Conrad's claim for sailors as "the grown-up children of a discontented earth."

Yachting, after all, consists of adrenalin panics slotted into eternities of dumb slogging. It is only our perception of that process that adds up to ecstasy. Racing or cruising ("doing extraordinary boat maintenance in exotic locations") expands the soul. There is a sense of awe in every landfall. The grace note of each sunset is a reminder of boating's ultimate quest: the exhilaration of feeling self-sufficient and the joy of opening oneself to new experiences. "Messing about in boats"

heals. It releases harried individuals from what Don Quixote mischievously called "the melancholy burden of sanity."

My favourite moment of any outing arrives when the day folds into itself and I'm heading for one of the Royal Vancouver Yacht Club's home docks or outstations. It is only when my boat is safely tied that I fully realize why the club means so much to me. It is a sanctuary. Great clubs are like that. They're family; you feel at home.

I return from even the briefest outing with heightened sensitivity. I see the world anew with a surge of inner excitement that the best of urban experiences can never match. What the club provides is validation of those feelings. Validated, because they're shared.

It is comforting to know that even if you walk into any club function and recognize few of the members present, you will be glad to meet them, just because you find them there. An essentially egalitarian spirit pervades the RVYC, both in its admission policies and club rules. The only taboo is never to put on airs or demand special privileges. Club membership grants us watery access to an empty ocean filled with wonders, and that's privilege enough.

Preface

This book is dedicated to the members of the Royal Vancouver Yacht Club, to the many volunteers who have given much to the institution and to their community over the last century, and to the staff, from general managers to the people at Jericho, Coal Harbour and the offshore stations. Without them, there would be no club.

THIS IS a selective, image-oriented history of the Royal Vancouver Yacht Club. It is not a comprehensive account of every event, personality, boat, crew, trophy and race. That detailed accounting of the club's history exists in the volumes of the *Annals of the Royal Vancouver Yacht Club,* which deal with all aspects of the club's history from 1903 to 1985. As well, there are volumes of the club's newsletter, known as the *Seabreeze* for the last fifty years, which provide an intimate accounting of the club's day-to-day activities.

The title of this book, *Racers and Rovers,* speaks to the shared love of racing and roving at sea found in any yacht club. More than that, this book celebrates the club's centennial in 2003; it is an account of its history for current and future members of the club, and for those members of the general public who are fascinated by the lore and romance of yachting, as well as how this particular club reflects its community on the western shore of Canada. It is a popular history, therefore, and by necessity it paints the canvas with a broad brush. I apologize in advance for anyone who feels that an important aspect of the club's history, or a particular person, has been either left out or not given sufficient due.

The writing of *Racers and Rovers* was made possible by the Centennial Book Committee of the Royal Vancouver Yacht Club, led by Honorary Historian Jock Ferrie, and was approved by the Executive Committees of the club, headed by then commodores Bill Botham and David Everett. I would also like to particularly thank Editorial Committee members Jock Ferrie, John Long, Brian O'Sullivan, Michael Scott, Paddy Thomson and Guy Walters—

and co-ordinator Jeff Bickerstaff—without whose time and effort this book would not have happened. Of note is the fact that both Jock Ferrie and Paddy Thomson are third-generation members of the club.

The book benefited from the in-club review of Bill Botham, Jock Ferrie, Bob Matthews, Brian O'Sullivan, Michael Scott, Paddy Thomson and Guy Walters, and archivists Donald Byrne (whose tireless efforts to collect and catalogue material continued right up to his death in October 2002) and Astrid Kenning, as well as researchers and proof-readers Bonar Davis, John Long, David Macdonald, Marylile Martin, John Purdy, Stephen Tupper, Guy Walters and Bill West. I also want to thank Vickie Jensen for her careful review and suggestions.

I would like to thank interviewees Gary Anderson, Alex Andrews, Jack Balmer, Lyall O. Bell, Bill Botham, Bruce Buchanan, Ted Chapman, J.V. "Jack" Christensen, Foster Dennison, John Dew, A. William Everett, A.J.B. Forsyth, Bob Gibson, Gordon Gibson, Milt Goodman, Philip Graham, Ted Jefferys, Bill Kidner, Bill Killam, Pat Leslie, Sue Liebert, John Long, Brian McDermott, Doug McPherson, Don Martin, Bob Matthews, David Miller, John Newton, Lynne Newton, Brian O'Sullivan, Ches Rickard, David Rolfe, Agnete Sandwell, Baird Tewksbury, Steve Tupper, Bill West, David Williams and Alex Wood. There is such a wealth of history and so many great stories in the interviews that they merit a book on their own, and I apologize for not being able to do each interview justice in the limited space available in this book.

This book would not have been possible without the RVYC's honorary historians, who saved the

history of the club as it made the transition from present to past, never an easy task in a fast-moving organization: George A. Cran, Jock Ferrie, Watson MacCrostie, Gerry Palmer and Gordon Warren. I also thank Andy Copeland, Kyly Killam, Wally Raepple, Baird Tewksbury and David Williams for their research and writing. Foster Dennison provided a wealth of photographs, documents and memorabilia, which also proved invaluable. Milt Goodman, the club's long-time photographer of activities, and Baird Tewksbury also provided images. And a special thank you to the club's General Manager Carmen Derricott for her great effort and support of the project.

As well, the following institutions and organizations were very helpful in finding the sources to help tell this story: the Royal Vancouver Yacht Club Archives, the Vancouver City Archives, the Vancouver Maritime Museum's W.B. and M.H. Chung Library, the Vancouver Public Library and the West Vancouver Memorial Library. I also thank the Seattle Yacht Club's historian and storyteller *par excellence*, Scott Rohrer, for sharing his research, and his thorough, compelling and humorous retelling of the Vancouver-Seattle controversy over the Dunsmuir Cup races of 1909.

In addition to the team at the Royal Vancouver Yacht Club, I am proud to have once again been associated with the Douglas & McIntyre team of editor Saeko Usukawa and designer George Vaitkunas.

Any errors or omissions are my own.

James P. Delgado

ON THE WATER

"Believe me, my young friend, there is nothing—absolute nothing—half so much worth doing as simply messing about in boats." – KENNETH GRAHAME, *THE WIND IN THE WILLOWS*

FOR AS LONG as people have traded, travelled and waged war on the seas, rivers and lakes of the globe, they have also used the water for recreation and to race in competition with one another. Once the sport and pastime of royalty, and then the privileged classes, these diversions on water have become, in the last decades, the pursuit of people from all walks of life. Romance still clings to the sport, but today the deck of a yacht is more likely to be claimed by a man or woman who is a working professional, a tradesperson or a student, rather than an independently wealthy "sportsman."

Even with all the pomp and circumstance of royal yacht clubs and yacht squadrons, and the famous names and famous boats and famous races and famous trophies, there remains, at the heart of it all, the sublime experience of pitting your all in an uncomfortable boat, built light and fast, as part of a team or as a determined individual. There is something in the human spirit that thrills to the idea of competing against another or against the limitations of one's self—and that essential part of our nature defines why we like sport in all its forms, including yachting, where the competition is also against another element, the sea itself. But there is also relaxation, reflection and tranquility; the ability to be your own captain, chart your own course, and cruise close to home or on a blue water passage. That is the essence of yachting: an opportunity to reach beyond the bonds of daily life ashore, to face a challenge or venture forth, if not for relaxation, then on a personal voyage.

William Cooper, one of England's avid yachtsman historians of the mid-nineteenth century, aptly pointed out that whether engaged in racing or cruising, "the true yachtsman is however common to both," and the diversity and range of experience, combined with the penchant for private clubs and associations, gave rise to an institution, the yacht club, that has spread throughout the world. This is the story of one club, its people, their boats and their community, all intertwined in a city on the sea.

For one hundred years, the Royal Vancouver Yacht Club (RVYC) has existed as an institution whose importance has been measured by many factors: the number of members and boats; the number of races and trophies; the types of activities; the quality and style of the clubhouses and offshore stations. But the greater indicator of its importance is its relationship with the community. In many ways the club is a reflection of Vancouver, as it was, and as it is. Born of maritime trade and commerce, Vancouver, whose motto is "By Sea, Land and Air We Prosper," naturally turns to the water for recreation and enjoyment. The city's oldest sports are sailing and rowing on the waters of Coal Harbour, English Bay and False Creek. In an age before professional sports, yachts and races on the water commanded the same attention from the press and public as a Canucks game.

But this is more than a story about a particular sport, or about boats, or an institution. This is a story about people and about the recreational aspects of the sea, a community in which the sea dominates the landscape, as well as the history and culture, commerce and industry. This is a story of people from many walks of life whose passion, or life, as many have explained it, "is boating." For these people, the Royal Vancouver Yacht Club has been another family, a favourite spot at which to gather for the love of the sport and recreation, and to socialize with others who share the common bond.

CHAPTER 1

RACERS AND ROVERS

These innovations have given rise to the designations of "Racing Yachtsmen," and "Cruising Yachtsmen."
The former appellation implying those who revel amidst huge spars, enormous spread of canvas,
and piles of lead ... whilst the latter denotes the quiet, comfort-loving rover of the sea, who loves sailing
for sailing's sake.... Sailing a match he regards in the same light as setting a chimney on fire in order
to have the fun of putting it out." –"VANDERDECKEN" (WILLIAM COOPER, ESQ.), 1873

THE SEA SURROUNDS and invades the Netherlands. Rivers and canals push into the heart of the lowlands and beyond into Germany and Belgium. Here, where the water defines the land, the concept of the yacht, born of the ancient tradition of a ship of state—the luxurious vessel of a ruler—found expression in Holland.

The word "yacht" comes from the sixteenth-century Dutch *jaght*, derived from *jaghen*, "to hunt or pursue" and the slang term that followed it, *jaghten*, "to hurry along." *Jaghts*, or *jaght schips*, were fast, light-built craft designed for war, and then adapted to commerce and, finally, pleasure. By the seventeenth century, the waterways of the Netherlands were crowded with ornately decorated, privately owned jaghts of the wealthy burgher classes made rich by a burgeoning overseas trade.

The English copied the form and function of these vessels, anglicizing the name to "yought" or "yaught," The word "yaught" was popularized after 1660 when the exiled King Charles II and his family, returned to power after Oliver Cromwell's death, sailed home in a Dutch jaght. Charles, captivated by the small and magnificently decorated

Facing page: Yachting spread beyond England as clubs were established around the world. A French club holds a *Regatta at Argenteuil* in 1893 in this oil on canvas scene by Gustave Caillebotte (1848–1894).
Private collection/Bridgeman Art Library BRM176785

The first English royal yachts at sea, modelled on a Dutch design, in a late seventeenth-century scene by artist Willem van de Velde the Younger (1633–1707).
Christie's Images/London, Bridgeman Art Library CH24025

The Word "Yacht"

Here is a definition of the word "yacht" from Falconer's *Dictionary of the Marine* (1780):
A vessel of state, normally employed to convey princes, ambassadors, and other great personages from one kingdom to another ... As the principal design of a yacht is to accommodate the passengers, it is usually fitted with a variety of convenient apartments, with suitable furniture, according to the quality or number of persons contained therein. The Royal Yachts are commonly rigged as Ketches, except the principal one reserved for the sovereign, which is equipped with three masts like a ship. They are generally elegantly furnished and nobly ornamented with sculpture, and always commanded by Captains in His Majesty's Navy. Besides these, there are many other yachts of a smaller kind, employed by the commissioners of excise, navy and customs; or used as pleasure boats by private gentlemen.

In the nineteenth century, yachting experienced phenomenal growth. In this painting (panel) by Nicholas Condy (1793–1857), a topsail schooner passes a schooner of the Royal Yacht Squadron off the coast of Dorset.
Bonhams, London, UK/Bridgeman Art Library
BON65388

vessel, praised it so volubly that his Dutch hosts gave him the yacht *Mary,* establishing the precedent for a long line of royal yachts.

Charles cruised the Thames in his yacht, adding to his fleet of pleasure vessels throughout his reign and then, when he grew tired of them, passing them on to the Royal Navy. Historians count "at least twenty-five other royal yachts between 1661 and 1685, which the king found he neither had the time, nor perhaps the inclination, to use himself." He also raced his yachts, but the races were sporadic and usually in competition with his brother, the Duke of York. Royal cruises also extended beyond the Thames across the English Channel, and after Charles II, English monarchs and their families used a progression of royal yachts in this fashion. Rulers of other nations also adopted the yacht, among them Peter the Great, Russia's great sailor tsar, who in 1718 established the world's first yacht club, the Flotilla of the Neva, in St. Petersburg.

The next yacht club, the Water Club of Cork, Ireland, was founded in 1720; its members cruised in formation, wore "splendid uniforms" and entertained lavishly. Three other yacht clubs established in the eighteenth century—the Lough Ree Yacht Club of Ireland (founded as the Athlone Yacht Club), the Starcross Yacht Club of Devon and the Royal Thames Yacht Club (founded in England as the Cumberland Fleet)—mark the beginning of yachting as something beyond the pastime of royalty; a pursuit of gentlemen, be they naval officers or merchants.

Yachting in Colonial Times
North American interest in yachting began in colonial times, particularly in and around New York. A 1717 engraving of New York harbour shows several yachts, though a history of the time notes that "racing on the water was not much in fashion, though the gentry had their barges, and some their yachts or pleasure boats." The continent's first yacht club, established at Halifax, Nova Scotia, in 1837, is now the Royal Nova Scotia Yacht Squadron.

The great age of yachting was launched, and the number of clubs exploded around the globe. In 1800, the world boasted four active yacht clubs; by 1844, there were thirty-three and by 1900, there were well over a hundred.

Yachting became the sport of
more than royalty in the
eighteenth century. The yachts
of the Cumberland Fleet are
starting on the Thames off
Blackfriars, London, in this
eighteenth-century oil on
canvas by the English School.
Royal Thames Yacht Club, London, UK/
Bridgeman Art Library BAL4918

Top: The royal yacht *Britannia*, built for the Prince of Wales (later King Edward VII) in 1893, was a famous racer that won 231 first prizes and 129 second or third prizes in 635 starts. After the king's death in 1935, *Britannia* was scuttled off the Isle of Wight.

From Hughes, *Famous Yachts*, published in 1928

Bottom: A page from a nineteenth-century sailing club album shows the old flags of some of Great Britain's first sailing clubs.

Royal Thames Yacht Club, London, UK/ Bridgeman Art Library PHD51599

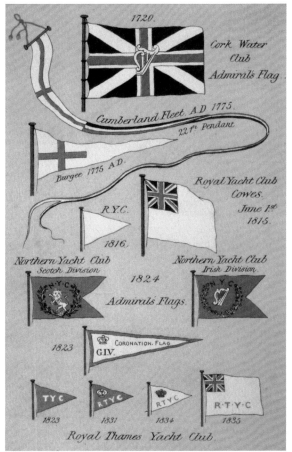

Canada's First Yacht Clubs

Royal Nova Scotia Yacht Squadron (1837)
Royal Canadian Yacht Club, Toronto (1852)
Bay of Quinte Yacht Club (1876)
Pointe Claire Yacht Club (1879)
Toronto Sailing & Canoe Club (1880)
Buffalo Canoe Club, Ontario (1882)
Royal Hamilton Yacht Club (1888)
Queen City Yacht Club (1889)
Royal Victoria Yacht Club (1892)
Saint John Yacht Club (1894)
Kingston Yacht Club, Ontario (1896)
Royal Kennebeccasis Yacht Club (1898)
Royal Cape Breton Yacht Club (1899)
Royal Vancouver Yacht Club (1903)
Royal Lake of the Woods Yacht Club (1903)

In 1830, Thomas Assheton-Smith of the Royal Yacht Squadron had commissioned Britain's first steam yacht, only to face such opposition that he was forced to leave the club because steam yachts "were regarded as even more ungentlemanly than hand-to-hand fighting during races." All of that changed after Queen Victoria's adoption of steam for her new royal yacht, *Victoria and Albert,* in 1842. From then on, large steam yachts became a symbol of wealth and luxury, introducing a new approach to cruising.

The other factor in the increased popularity of yachts and yachting was the rise of the regatta, international competitions in which clubs from around the world met to compete in races. Yachting became *the* international sport, a matter of national pride, and while a sport played by the wealthy and noble, the general populace followed it with interest. Yachts, yacht clubs and yachtsmen were the sporting heroes of the Victorian and Edwardian age. *Britannia,* with its owner, the Prince of Wales, as a member of the crew, won 157 prizes in 219 races between 1892 and 1897, a signal achievement and a matter of British pride in an era in which a nautical dictionary defined yachting first as "the sport of racing in yachts and boats with sails for money or plate," and only second as "the pastime of cruising for pleasure in sailing or steam vessels."

THE AMERICA'S CUP
The race that catapulted yachting into a scene of international competition was held at Cowes, off the Isle of Wight, in 1851. The 101-foot yacht

The America's Cup, first raced for in 1851, became yachting's most fabled trophy and the subject of intense competition. *Rounding Benton Reef Light-ship,* during an early contest for the cup, was depicted by artist Fred Cozzens in 1883.

The Regatta

Originally a Venetian term for races between the city's fabled gondolas, the regatta spread internationally to mean any competition between rowed craft, like that held at Dieppe in 1837 as France's first "regatta." Within a few years, the concept and the term were expanded to include races between sailing craft, and today, a regatta is a formally organized race under sail.

The annual regatta at Cowes, off the Isle of Wight in the English Channel, organized by the Royal Yacht Squadron, became the highlight of the yachting season, particularly after 1864, when Edward, Prince of Wales, competed. This ushered in a twenty-year period in which the future king actively raced in seven different yachts, culminating with his last and favourite yacht, *Britannia,* laid down in 1892 when he was commodore of the Royal Yacht Squadron. Royal patronage—and the participation of other royalty—Kaiser Wilhelm II of Germany, Tsar Nicholas of Russia and King Alfonso of Spain, and the attendant publicity they brought, introduced yachting not only into the lifestyles of those who desired to be part of the inner circle but also brought it to the attention of the masses.

Sir Thomas Lipton, a perennial challenger for the America's Cup, was a sportsman par excellence and the sponsor of the Lipton Cup(s). His famous yacht, the America's Cup contender, *Shamrock I* (built in 1898), was the first of five *Shamrock*s to race for Lipton until his death in 1931.

From Hughes, *Famous Yachts*, published in 1928

America, owned by a syndicate headed by John C. Stevens of the New York Yacht Club, sailed to Cowes at the invitation of the Royal Yacht Squadron. The British challenged her crew to a race with fourteen of their yachts around the Isle of Wight for a "100 Guinea Cup" of sterling silver. *America* won the race and the cup, which went to the United States "to be preserved as a perpetual challenge cup for friendly competition between foreign countries." Known now as the America's Cup, the trophy began a century and a half series of challenges and continues to attract the best designers, the best yachts and enormous sums of money. The obsession with the cup was exemplified in the late nineteenth century by Britain's quest to regain it, particularly the efforts of grocery and tea merchant Sir Thomas Lipton from 1899 to 1930. Five times, and at great cost, Lipton raced for the cup, in the process, and "in no small way due to his own efforts," making the competition for the America's Cup "the most prestigious racing event in the world."

The initial rules of the Royal Yacht Squadron were expanded in the aftermath of the loss of the "100 Guinea Cup" to *America* and a series of controversies over how to properly measure and rate a yacht. Various "measurement rules" were introduced, and yacht designers responded by finding ways around the rules to find a competitive edge. Whether a yacht was a "rule-cheater" or not occupied a great deal of attention and led to discord between clubs. In 1875, the Yacht Racing Association was formed to deal with the situation, but controversy remained a part of competition, adding both to the flavour and to the appeal of yachting for the masses. To have a yacht club, and to follow the sport, was a source of pride and great interest for a community, as much as a hockey or football franchise is today. So it was that organized yachting reached the edge of the forests of British Columbia.

Kaiser Wilhelm of Germany was, like his uncle Edward VII, an inveterate yachtsman. *Germania* and *Meteor IV* were the first of the kaiser's yachts designed, built and crewed entirely by Germans. Wilhelm was an arrogant and highly competitive racer who so irked Edward VII at Cowes one year that the king gave up racing.

From Hughes, *Famous Yachts,* published in 1928

CHAPTER 2

"WE SHOULD NOT BE ATTACHED TO ANYONE'S TOWLINE"

"Why should the yachtsmen of Victoria show us the lead...? We should not be attached to anyone's towline in this fashion. The boats that are now in commission and those being completed would form a first-class club, if the owners and yachtsmen generally, would co-operate to advance the interests of the sport." —VANCOUVER WORLD, 27 MARCH 1902

BORN OF VOLCANIC FIRE, sculpted by ice and flooded at the end of the last great ice age as the glaciers retreated, British Columbia's coast is an intricate maze of fjords, islands and sounds. These waters, protected from the open Pacific Ocean by the intervening mass of Vancouver Island, formed a highway on which the First Nations and subsequent visitors from across the seas travelled, traded and settled. The sea has shaped and influenced the development of what is now British Columbia from the beginning of human history in this part of the world and provides a unique and world-renowned setting for recreational boating that has inspired the formation of several yacht clubs.

The phenomenon of the yacht club gained popularity just as the global tide of urbanization and industrialization reached the Pacific shores of the North American continent. Following the discovery of gold in California in 1848, and the subsequent discovery of gold in British Columbia in 1858, cities began to rise in what was still considered the wilderness—despite thousands of years of earlier settlement by the First Nations.

The formal establishment of yacht clubs came as each metropolis matured, and the concept of sport and recreation took hold. Not surprisingly, the first yacht club on the Pacific Coast, the San Francisco Yacht Club, was founded in 1869.

Facing page: Breezing along in light airs on English Bay.
Vancouver Maritime Museum

The early settlers on Burrard Inlet loved to take to the water for recreation. A well-dressed group poses in a motley collection of boats and canoes on Seymour Creek in the late nineteenth century.
Vancouver City Archives Out.N.2.P.91

Other clubs on the Pacific followed: Santa Barbara (1872), the Corinthian Yacht Club of San Francisco (1886), San Diego (1886), and then, in 1892, in Encinal, Seattle, Anacortes, New Whatcom and Victoria.

The establishment of a yacht club in Victoria came as the result of a direct challenge from nearby American yacht clubs in the State of Washington, whose boats sailed, unannounced, into Victoria for the annual 24 May Queen's Birthday celebrations, which included a sailing race. The four visiting American boats challenged the Victoria boats and won the top prizes. Within two days, the *Victoria Times* reported that a group of citizens had decided to form a yacht club "on a scale commensurate with the size and importance" of British Columbia's capital city. By 1 July, the first boats from Victoria to challenge the Americans sailed across the Strait of Georgia to race at Anacortes. While the Canadians did not win, they demonstrated that they were ready to join in the fun—and to provide what all hoped would be some first-class international competi-

Hastings Mill in 1886, on the eve of the birth of Vancouver, was a rough and tumble mill town. On this working waterfront and on these waters (shown here is Coal Harbour), recreational boating was born on Burrard Inlet.

Vancouver City Archives Mi.N.28.P.35

tion. On 25 August 1892, representatives from all of the clubs founded the Northwest International Yachting Association.

YACHTING ON BURRARD INLET

What was missing was participation from a newly founded city, also in Canadian waters, that had begun to challenge Victoria for supremacy as the province's great port. Just incorporated as Vancouver, the tiny settlement on the shores of Burrard Inlet had already grown from a logging camp boasting all of fifty residents in 1870 to a city of fifteen thousand by 1892. But the idea of recreational boating was not a foreign concept to its denizens. From the start of settlement, when time was available after the day's work was done, people took pleasure in boating on English Bay or Burrard Inlet, as well as the Fraser River.

Vancouver was originally two settlements. The first was Hastings Mill, a small "company town" managed since 1882 by R.H. Alexander, a Scottish emigrant who had hiked overland to participate in

Early holidays and civic events in Vancouver usually featured sport on the water, such as this Dominion Day regatta in Coal Harbour in 1890.

Vancouver City Archives Bo.P.109

the 1862 Cariboo gold rush before arriving in 1869 at the mill to work as an accountant. The other settlement, Granville, established outside the boundaries of the "dry" company town, was a saloon-centred, lively collection of buildings nicknamed "Gastown" for its verbose founder, "Gassy" Jack Deighton. The small settlement grew because it provided food, booze, prostitutes and other more mundane but essential services, like a Chinese laundry, to the loggers and mill hands who were bachelors without ready access to meals, a good time or laundry service, as well as those who didn't care much for Mr. Alexander's company rules at Hastings Mill. But the two settlements were destined to merge, with the inevitable conflict of

lifestyles. In 1884, the Canadian Pacific Railway (CPR) selected Granville as the terminus of the transcontinental railroad in exchange for a grant of 6,458 acres of real estate. The new town site, named Vancouver by the CPR, was bound to grow once the rails met the sea and the CPR's transpacific steamers commenced regular service.

The town's early leaders established a sense of community through patriotic celebrations and organized sports. R.H. Alexander put together some of the settlement's first boat races off the Hastings Mill dock around 1882. These first regattas were between rowboats, with four-oared craft competing. The shouts of bystanders, oars flashing through the water and the strain on faces giving way to exultation

The earliest racers on Burrard Inlet were small sloops and cats.
Vancouver Maritime Museum

Commodore R.H. Alexander strikes a nautical pose in his official portrait.

or despair ultimately inspired the creation of the Vancouver Boating Club in 1886 and the Burrard Inlet Rowing Club in 1890 to train, organize and compete. But sailing competitions also took place, and the formation of a sailing club was not far off.

The first sailing race out of Vancouver reported by the press was on Sunday, 6 June 1886. A new "pleasure yacht," *Senor,* built by Messrs. Nelson and Hansen of Hastings Mill, outdistanced the sloop *Marcia.* On Sunday, 25 June, in another race, Alderman Peter Cordiner's boat *Effie* "outstripped all competition" when *Senor*'s crew gave up and *Marcia* was left in third place. All through the "season" that extended until 25 September, reports of water races filled the newspapers, proposing regattas from the Carrall Street Wharf to Bowen Island and back "for a flag."

By mid-May 1887, the *Advertiser* reported that Burrard Inlet was "covered" from English Bay to Port Moody "with all kinds of sailing craft." On 27 May, a meeting to organize the "large number of sailing craft" led to the formation of the Burrard Inlet Sailing Club, with sixteen charter members pledging to build a slip, floating wharf and boathouse. The chairman was Henry O. Bell-Irving, a civil engineer who had arrived to survey the region for the CPR and decided to stay on. Now the owner of a successful import business, "H.O." was a member of the new city elite and an avid yachtsman. By 8 June, the new club's membership stood at over thirty and plans for a regatta that "promises to be the most interesting feature of the day" were afoot for the Queen's Jubilee celebrations on 1 July. Thereafter, regattas followed every 1 July, as well as for the Queen's Birthday celebrations on 24 May. The number of yachts increased, all of them owned by the city's most prominent citizens.

THE DEMISE OF THE FIRST CLUBS

The Burrard Inlet Sailing Club did not last long, however, and neither did a number of other short-lived clubs. "One of these included most of the tugboat skippers," according to early RVYC historian Gordon Warren. They "used to hold club meetings on some convenient pier head, seated on fender piles and odd coils of rope, from which they directed the affairs of the club, much to the disgust of the amateur sailors." With the demise of the clubs,

Richard Henry (R.H.) Alexander (*left*), standing on the porch of his office, was the manager of Hastings Mill around 1890. He was also an early booster of recreational boating and the second commodore of the Royal Vancouver Yacht Club.

Vancouver City Archives Mi.P.46.N.35

Recreational boating is usually accompanied by a good sense of humour. It certainly is evident in this early scene on Coal Harbour.

Above: Roving the waters of Burrard Inlet in a steam launch off Brockton Point in 1893 were a party of men and women—many of whom later joined the Vancouver Yacht Club. They are identified on the photo as "Edward Mahon, Mrs. W.E. Graveley, Mrs. Lewis (later Mrs. W. Barlee), Miss Nellie Cambie (later Mrs. Neville F. Townsend), Henry Mahon, McIvor (Puffy) Campbell, T.H. Calland, Charles Henshaw, Mrs. Henshaw, Miss Ethel Moore (later Mrs. J.C. Donald), Sid Williams, and Mr. Tingley."

Right: Regattas and races filled the waters off Vancouver during the young city's "Regatta and Carnival" of 31 August to 5 September 1896.

Vancouver Maritime Museum

OFFICIAL
SOUVENIR PROGRAMME
of
1896
VANCOUVER
REGATTA and CARNIVAL
AUGUST 31ST To SEPT. 5TH

PRINTED BY THE
NEWS-ADVERTISER

Walter Graveley headed up a group that founded the B.C. Yacht Racing Association, but that did not last long either, as the worst economic depression of the nineteenth century hit Vancouver hard between 1893 and 1896.

As the depression ground on, hope for Vancouver came in 1897 with the discovery of gold in the Yukon Territory. Entrepreneurs exhorted investment in the city, now touted as the "gateway to the Klondike," with steamship departures up the Inside Passage to hastily erected ports on formerly uninhabited northern inlets as the jumping-off points to the gold fields. In this optimistic environment, a group of local yachtsmen, led by R.Y. Ellis, C. Gardner Johnson and Walter Graveley, founded the Vancouver Yacht Club. Graveley, viewed as Vancouver's most enthusiastic yachtsman, offered the new club space in a building he owned. Andy Linton, a pioneer boat builder and an avid yachtsman in his own right, with a renowned fast yacht,

May, provided slips at his float at the foot of Carrall Street. It made sense for the new club to be associated with Linton, as it was to him both "swells" and workingmen went when they wanted to rent a boat. In Vancouver, back then, the "centre of the universe was Andy's wharf."

Unfortunately, despite being at the centre of the universe, the Vancouver Yacht Club also languished. After a few years without a club, but with a number of fervent yachtsmen in the city, the time was ripe for another try. Vancouver had gained several other clubs at the end of the century, such as the Vancouver Club, the Terminal City Club, and the Vancouver Lawn and Tennis

Founding Members and Boats of the Vancouver Yacht Club, 1903

Commodore Walter E. Graveley: 20-foot keel cabin sloop *Margot*
Vice-Commodore William Hodson: open deck yawl *Frolic*
Rev. John Antle: sloop *Laverock*
Albert Austin: 19-foot open cat-boat *Addie*
Paddy Cambie: 27-foot Columbia River centerboard sloop *Pirate*
Austin French: 33-foot cabin yawl *Trixie*
Alexander Grant: 30-foot half-deck clinker built sloop *Siren*, and a 16-foot flush deck sloop *Glendochart*
Albert J. Hancock: 25-1/2-foot sloop *Petrel*
Mr. Hooper: sloop *Norma*
Hilton Keith: 20-foot half-deck sloop *Maple Leaf*
Gordon Legg: lugger *Waterwag*
William McDougall: centerboard sloop *Rob Roy*
Oswald Moseley: 25-foot keel cabin sloop *Thelma*
H.W. Robertson: 19-foot centerboard sloop *Rip Rip*
E.W. Stark: sloop *Alpha*
Philip N. Thompson: 35-foot auxiliary cruising yawl *Bertha*
Arthur G. Thynne: 35-foot yawl *Golliwog*
W.H. Billings
C.S.V. Branch
A.E. Bull
A.C. Burdick
W.B. Ferrie
C.B. MacNeill
R.G. McPherson
J.H. Senkler
O.L. Spencer
C.H. Usborne

Facing page: On the early Vancouver waterfront, boat builder
Andy Linton's craft were always
available for sale or hire.

Vancouver City Archives Port.P. 1664.N.333

Andy Linton's boathouse at the
foot of Carrall Street, around
1889–90. At the dock are the
yacht *St. Patrick*, a cat boat,
and the yachts *Laurleen* and
May, the latter the fastest yacht
on Burrard Inlet "until the spoon
bow came."

Vancouver City Archives Bo.N.63.P.102

WALTER E. GRAVELEY

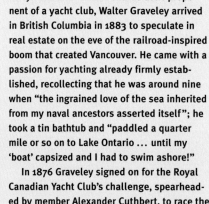

Early Vancouver's most enthusiastic proponent of a yacht club, Walter Graveley arrived in British Columbia in 1883 to speculate in real estate on the eve of the railroad-inspired boom that created Vancouver. He came with a passion for yachting already firmly established, recollecting that he was around nine when "the ingrained love of the sea inherited from my naval ancestors asserted itself"; he took a tin bathtub and "paddled a quarter mile or so on to Lake Ontario ... until my 'boat' capsized and I had to swim ashore!"

In 1876 Graveley signed on for the Royal Canadian Yacht Club's challenge, spearheaded by member Alexander Cuthbert, to race the New York Yacht Club for the vaunted America's Cup. Cuthbert's hastily completed schooner *Countess of Dufferin* horrified the New Yorkers, who took themselves and their club, not to mention the cup, very seriously. The press sniffed derisively that the Canadian yacht had sails "set like a purser's shirt on a handspike" and a hull "as rough as a nutmeg grater." Nevertheless, the dauntless Canadian challengers pressed on to race but lost twice to the yacht *Madeleine* in a three-race competition. The third race never happened; New York authorities seized *Countess of Dufferin* for Cuthbert's debts, and a few days later,

before the sheriff realized what was happening, the Canadians slipped out to sea and fled the long arm of Yankee law.

Graveley moved west and eventually ended up in Vancouver, where, during the great fire of June 1886, he dashed into the heart of the burning district to retrieve what he could from his office. The town was an inferno, with wind-whipped flames engulfing buildings and people in an instant, and sap-soaked trees exploding into fireballs. Grabbing what he could, Graveley ran past a man with a group of children who begged him for help. Without pausing, Graveley picked up a child, hoisted it on his shoulders and raced through the flames to the shores of False Creek.

Graveley became a key figure in Vancouver's yachting community, and in 1903 organized the meeting that created a new club, which, by the end of his tenure as founding commodore, had gained the royal warrant to become the Royal Vancouver Yacht Club. Named Honorary Life Commodore in 1907, he remained an active member until his death in 1939. In keeping with his love of the sea and yachting, Walter Graveley's ashes were committed to the waters of English Bay in August 1939 from Commodore Harold A. Jones's yacht *Spirit*.

Top: Real estate speculator and keen boater Walter Graveley served as the first commodore of the Royal Vancouver Yacht Club.

Bottom: Walter Graveley's office, on Cambie Street, was the setting for the founding meeting of the Vancouver Yacht Club in 1903.
Vancouver City Archives STR.P.222.N.135

The yacht *Syren*, built by Captain William Watts, off Vancouver's Evans Coleman Dock at the foot of Abbott Street around 1891. That year, *Syren* won the first international yacht race on the Pacific coast when she raced to victory, with Watts at the helm, against the Americans at Bellingham's Fairhaven.

Top: *Wideawake*, racing with Bun and Evans, the sons of E.B. "Jimmy" Deane, on 24 May 1911.

Bottom: On a grey and blustery day in early Vancouver, the city's boaters take to the inlet while onlookers watch from shore.

Vancouver Maritime Museum

The Vancouver Yacht Club's earliest sailors included the women of the young city. Three ladies pause on a row to shore.

Club. The impetus for the new yacht club, interestingly enough, came not from within the community, but from outside the country.

THE SEATTLE CHALLENGE

The Seattle yachting community, which with its sister clubs had crossed Juan de Fuca Strait to galvanize Victoria into action, spurred Vancouver through the *Seattle Times.* The American sailors were eager for international competition, the more the merrier. While the *Seattle Times* stirred the pot, so too did the *Vancouver World.* On 27 March 1902, the *World* reported that Mr. Oswald Moseley of Vancouver had launched a new yacht, *Thelma,* from the Watts yard in Coal Harbour: "A few more enthusiastic and consistent yachting men such as Mr. Moseley, will soon raise the sport of yachting in Vancouver from its present stagnant state." The *World* upped the ante on 25 December, when its sports editor announced that Vancouver had no yachts capable of "competing with those of Seattle or Victoria." Those were fighting words. The next day, the *World* published a letter from Vancouver yachtsman V.M. Dafoe: "Well, sir, I wish to state that in a cruising race from Port Townsend to Seattle in

the *Halcyon,* with the winning yacht of the international race there in 1900, I arrived so far ahead that they refused to accept my challenge for another race. I am willing to sail the *Halcyon,* or any smaller boat also of my design, with any boats of equal rating in British Columbia or Puget Sound waters."

Prodded and stung by the press, seventeen Vancouver yachtsmen, again led by Walter Graveley, described by the *Seattle Times* as "the Daddy of them all in the Vancouver yachting world," met on the evening of 5 February 1903, and agreed to form a new Vancouver Yacht Club. The group elected the irrepressible Graveley as its first commodore. Among the various tasks that faced the club, in addition to the inevitable bylaws and a headquarters, was the burning issue of a challenge to Seattle.

The press warmly greeted the news. The *Vancouver Daily Ledger* announced that "The Vancouver Yacht Club is the name of a healthy young infant that was born into the amateur world of sport last night." The stage was now set for Vancouver to make its first foray into the international racing community.

CHAPTER 3

Achievement, Acclaim and International Controversy

"Naturally gifted with a cruising ground of wonderful charm and unrivalled in the extent of protected tidal waters within easy reach of the yachtsman, besides the great Pacific Ocean beyond; it is not surprising that the Royal Vancouver Yacht Club, with its base at British Columbia's principal seaport, should have gathered under its burgee a large fleet of pleasure craft." —CLUB HISTORIAN GORDON B. WARREN, 1931

VANCOUVER'S NEW YACHT CLUB immediately focused on a race with Seattle. It was not a challenge undertaken lightly; the new club's members proposed building six challengers, at a cost of about $400 each, which was then a great deal of money. Yacht racing was definitely either a rich man's sport, or the result of a consortium or syndicate of investors pitching in. The boats were to be built to a model that would "enable them to be cabin topped and converted into cruisers after they had served their purpose as racers." Once built, the six boats would be selected "by lots" by different sailing crews, and local races would select the top boat that would be "pitted against the Victoria and Seattle flyers to compete in the international race." After the race, the six yachts would "be sold to the highest bidder at auction among the club members

for cruising purposes, and the proceeds divided pro rata among those" who had funded the construction; "thus a new set of six racers will be built each year."

While dreams of international glory occupied the new club's attention, more mundane matters also weighed on their minds. Vancouver was still a logging town, and club members complained that log booms were endangering their yachts, anchored in Coal Harbour near downtown. In May 1903, the club protested the "promiscuous floating logs in the harbour" that were bumping up against boats and buoys, causing "no end of inconvenience."

GROWING PAINS

Another mundane matter was the need for a clubhouse. The club asked Albert "Bert" Austin, who was also a member of the Vancouver Rowing Club,

A black diamond on a Cambridge blue background was the original burgee for the Vancouver Yacht Club. This burgee, the sole survivor from the original fleet, was donated to the club by Oswald Moseley, a charter member in 1903 who was named an honorary life member in 1966.

Facing page: Burgee fluttering in the breeze, and sail and steam yachts alongside, the first clubhouse rests on its floats in Coal Harbour, circa 1904.

"to see if we could put a small float next to and tie up to and use the Rowing Club entrance, which was at the west end of the CPR wharf," at the foot of Bute Street. The Rowing Club obliged, "for a small fee, and they were a great help ... I never heard any kicks from the Rowing Club regarding the Yachtsmen," Austin later recalled, but by May, just three months after its founding, the yacht club's membership and fleet had grown, and "more accommodation has become a matter of necessity." Some members wanted to stay close to downtown, but others, like H.O. Alexander, son of R.H. Alexander of Hastings Mill, wanted to move to Jericho, an isolated section of beachfront a few miles out of town, because "the anchorage is fine and the position sheltered and far from the turmoil of city life."

The discussions over what to do continued for the next year while the number of members and boats grew quickly. By May, the club boasted eighteen boats, and the press reported "when the manifold joys of the sport are revealed to many of those who have no boats now, it is expected that there will be a substantial increase in the fleet of the club." That first year, the yachting season started with cruises over the May holiday weekend, with a "great time" as members sailed on two to three-day excursions. Vancouver's yachtsmen tested their sea legs in conditions that the papers reported as "rough weather in abundance, a little rain and much calm." The "degree of success," the press noted, was "determined by the individual likes and dislikes of those on board."

The club's first organized race, on 8 August 1903, was another matter of how one defined success. The race started that Saturday afternoon with "a score of yachts and many other craft lying off the beach. The weather was perfect, not a cloud being in the sky and an eight-mile wind blowing ... The white-clad yachtsmen and yachtswomen, the white sails and the different colored boats moving back and forward on the green water that sparkled in the sun was a picture long to be remembered," according to the press. But the race, for a cup presented to the club as a trophy by Vice-Commodore William Hodson, did not go according to plan.

The route, laid out as a triangle marked by buoys, was an eight-mile course that had to be completed within a four-hour limit. With the echo

The Coal Harbour fleet on the water in 1905.

A TOUGH DAY'S SAILING IN 1904

On 6 June 1904, the *Vancouver Province* reported that yachting the previous day had been "strenuous," with a capsizing and a stranding. The capsized yacht, *Maple Leaf*, a 20-foot yawl, came to grief off Point Atkinson Light. The yacht *Pirate*, sailing nearby, rescued the five-man crew of *Maple Leaf*, plucking them off the keel. The *Province* gleefully reported that the heroic crew of *Pirate* had themselves not sailed "without incident." The story continued:

Mr. A.E. Quigley was at the helm for a while, though it seemed all too long for Mr. [A.E.] Suckling, and an early disaster was all but recorded. The steamer *Danube* was sighted a mile away and Mr. Suckling, who was on the lookout, passed the word to the man at the wheel to give her plenty of room.

"That's all right," said Mr. Quigley. "Belay your talk there. We have right-of-way, and she's got to keep off. If she runs us down we can get damages."

"If we get run down," answered Mr. Suckling, as he hitched up his trousers in a nautical way and said "shiver me timbers, we shall certainly get damaged. Luff, you lubber, luff." Mr. Suckling did not know what luff meant, but it sounded right.

They sailed along and right enough Mr. Quigley brought the *Pirate* right across the bow of the *Danube*. When the big vessel seemed about a foot away Mr. Suckling roared, "Pull the blooming rudder stick."

"We have right of way," answered Mr. Quigley, becoming somewhat disturbed himself. "Tell them to turn."

"Right of way be hanged," said Mr. Suckling, "she's got the weight," and he jumped for the tiller. Mr. [F.B.] Springer eventually got the boat in safely and Mr. Suckling refused to play any more until Mr. Quigley was disrated.

Uwhilna was the club's flagship under second Commodore R.H. Alexander.

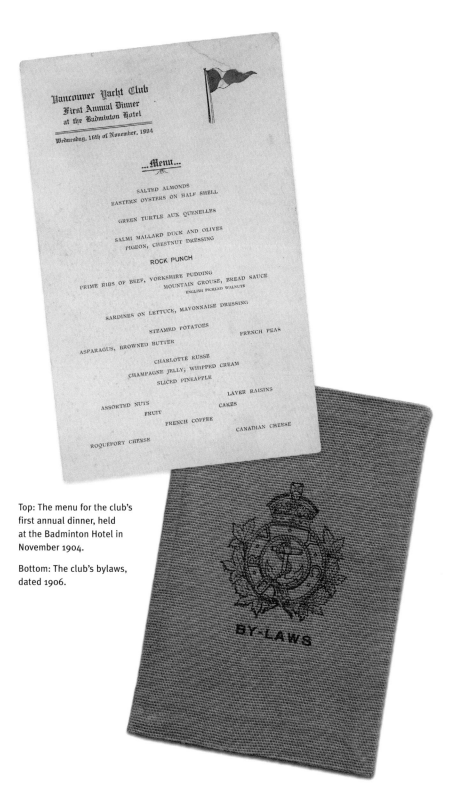

Top: The menu for the club's first annual dinner, held at the Badminton Hotel in November 1904.

Bottom: The club's bylaws, dated 1906.

of the starting gun resounding across the water, a fishing boat turned racer, W.H. Billings's *Mischief,* and several other boats headed for the first mark, well ahead of the rest of the pack. Unfortunately for Billings and his group, the wind died as they passed Stanley Park, and they "were consequently out of the race." When the rest of the fleet, led by Arthur Thynne's *Golliwog,* saw that the other boats were becalmed, they elected to first go to the second mark. Rounding their buoy, the group then made several short tacks and headed for the first mark, only to be "considerably surprised to discover that it was not in sight. The yachts flitted around a bit, and finally Walter Graveley, sailing *Golliwog,* spied it. The thing had turned turtle, and the little fishes were playing with the flag."

Alerted by Graveley, the group tacked and headed for the third mark, only to find that it had blown ashore, and so Graveley gybed and headed for the finish line, pursued by the remainder of the fleet. Letting his jib go forward to catch the wind, he watched in dismay as the sheet broke, "being too short to allow the spinnaker to be so carried, the boom was carried away, and *Golliwog* went over the line without the sail." Only four crossed the finish line; the others dropped out as soon as they discovered that "it would be no race." "Had it

Ailsa, Wideawake, Spirit, Golliwog, Britannia and an unidentified boat racing on English Bay, around 1912.
RVYC, A.H. Jefferd Collection

not provided a whole lot of fun anyway," said the newspapers, the race "would have been a failure. While the race was more like a fox and hound chase than a yachting contest, it was nevertheless a success for it brought out sixteen starters, and provided any amount of excitement." The following week, with better secured buoys, a fresh run of the failed race brought more satisfactory results.

THE CLUB EXPANDS

By the end of the club's first year, it had doubled in size, and the press reported: "Judging by the rapid increase in the membership and the many fine additions to the fleet, it will not be long before the club occupies a most prominent position among the clubs of the coast." The growth of the club outstripped the temporary quarters in the Vancouver Rowing Club, and, despite debate over staying close by or moving to the shores of English Bay, the members decided to stay downtown and build their own clubhouse. In March 1904, the *Vancouver Province* reported that the members had approved plans for their own building: "No better evidence of the enthusiasm and devotion to the sport on the part of local yachtsmen is needed."

To raise the money for the new clubhouse, some of the club's founders paid a $50 fee to become life members: "Over $800 was subscribed by twelve members . . . and other large amounts are also forthcoming shortly." The $50 fee granted a lifetime membership for what amounted to five years' dues at the rate of $10 per year. The first life members were: C.S.V. Branch, George C. Bushby, E.B. Deane, Austin French, Walter E. Graveley, Alexander Grant, William Hodson, M.H. Leggatt, Oswald Moseley, C.C. McCaul, K.C., J.H. Senkler, K.C., Arthur G. Thynne, P.N. Thompson, W.E. Thompson and W.B. Ferrie. Nearly half of them were founding officers: Commodore Graveley, Vice-Commodore Hodson, Fleet Captain Branch, and management committee members French, Senkler and Thynne. In 1966, the club honoured the only surviving subscriber, Oswald Moseley, with an honorary life membership, noting that his original $50 investment had "paid off more than handsomely." Cash was tight in 1904, and Moseley "probably took a long look at his $50 before be bought a life membership," but ultimately his "original fifty has given him membership . . . for less than $1 per year . . . the canny salt made an investment any market player might envy."

The new 30-by-60 foot structure was planned as a floating two-storey building, moored in Coal Harbour at the foot of Bute Street. "The lower part

"Wing on wing," *Alexandra*
catches the wind in 1904.
RVYC, Barney L. Johnson Collection

will be used for storing yachting gear, small dories and other paraphernalia, while comfortable quarters for the members will be fitted up on the upper floor. Reading, model and meeting rooms will be provided," while a "long landing" would run out to deep water "and the largest yachts will be enabled to tie up at any stage of the tide. There is good anchorage in front of the clubhouse, and the riding grounds are well sheltered from the rough water." Work on the new clubhouse was finished in June 1904, and members eagerly moved into their new quarters. By then, membership stood at 118, with a fleet of 38 boats, "not counting other boats under course of construction." Little did they realize that within a year the new clubhouse would be too small.

The club's first decade saw continued growth and a number of other significant developments. In 1904, the club gained its first motor vessel when sugar magnate B.T. Rogers joined with his steam yacht *Mow Ping.* Rogers had ordered the 50-foot yacht from A.S. Gordon & Co. of Hong Kong in 1899, stipulating, "I would like the boat named the *Po Ping* or *Mo Ping,* whichever means foreign devil." The yacht arrived in 1901 as *Mow Ping,* which literally means "without a pigtail," and thus a non-Chinese person.

The magazine *The Motor Boat* reported that interest in motorboats in Canada was rapidly

increasing, particularly on the Pacific Coast, "one of the finest cruising waters in the world... It is said that small craft about 30 feet in length may cruise from Vancouver to Alaska, a distance of about two thousand miles, in sheltered water. The growth of the sport has been very rapid in British Columbia, particularly in view of the sparseness of the population." It also noted that the Vancouver Yacht Club "is said to have the largest fleet of any on the Pacific coast. It includes the following motor craft: *Mow Ping,* B.T. Rogers; *Electra,* R.H. Sperling; *Arrow,* George H. Robinson; *Ariel,* George E. Bower; *Agnes,* Dr. Bell-Irving; *Roamer,* John S. Gall; *Gypsy,* W.J. Taaffe; *Tillie,* G.A. Roedde; *Valora,* E. Baker; *Icola,* A.B. Cook; *Mignonne,* Henry Darling; *Juanita,* W.C. Woodrow; *Camosun,* J.N. Henderson; *Aileen,* H.D. Hulme; *Beth,* R.P. McLennan." The club's requirements for joining with a motorboat were simple: "The committee have no restrictions whatever on your entry provided she is a cruiser, and carries a dinghy, life preservers, also lights and two anchors."

FIERCE COMPETITION

Motorboats notwithstanding, the heart and soul of the club remained the fierce competition between sailing yachts and other clubs. Racing on English Bay for the Commodore's Cup, a piece of silver donated by Walter Graveley, as well as the Hodson Cup, gave rise to trophies for every type of race and circumstances. In 1902, one of them, the Mackie Trophy, inspired the yachtsmen of Seattle to push Vancouver to form a club and compete for it. Sponsored by an English firm, the Mackie Trophy was a stuffed goat's head, which, in all its scruffy majesty, was an international yacht racing trophy that became hotly contested. In 1904, the trophy brought the Puget Sound, Port Townsend, Victoria and Nanaimo yachting communities to Vancouver to sail for it. Shortly after being founded, the Vancouver Yacht Club had joined the Northwest International Yacht Racing Association (NWIYRA) to participate in international races. The NWIYRA hosted regattas and events throughout the region, meaning that a yachtsman could spend the season in active competition and touring.

The club also organized weekend cruises for recreation: on 11–12 June 1904, some twenty boats set out up Burrard Inlet's North Arm to Bedwell Bay, a close and yet isolated spot for a retreat. "There are some eighty members of the club who do not yet own interests in yachts, and the idea of the cruise is to have all these members allotted to different vessels to take part in the cruise. A large tent will be taken up on a tug, which will also act as supply boat, and sleeping quarters for the overflow from the yacht bunks will be arranged on shore." The tent, also used as the mess, hosted a "clambake and smoke" on Saturday, with singing and a "smoker" that lasted into the night. By 1904, it was clear, the new yacht club was "A lively and integral part of Vancouver's sporting and social life."

The club was also part of a rapidly changing harbour. The crowded and increasingly industrial Coal Harbour waterfront surrounded the clubhouse with a number of boat builders and shipyards, and so in 1905, the club's executive applied to the park commissioners for a new spot, on the opposite shore. Granted in late 1905, the new site, in the lee of Deadman's Island, provided a respite. In 1906, when the government of Canada regranted the Stanley Park lands to the city, it made a provision for both the yacht and rowing clubs to have "exclusive use" of a portion of the park's foreshore.

Vancouver's growth and prosperity brought in more club members. The new middle class was buoyed by the financial boom at the beginning of the century, and the introduction of the five-day work week provided opportunities for weekend recreation, while the long summer days provided the chance for a sail on English Bay after work. Not every member was well off, as is evident in the tale of the first boat owned by the Cao brothers, Cliff, Reek and Chris. Launched in 1906, their boat, a centreboard sloop, was named *Swipe* by the brothers because "they swiped the lumber from Hastings Mill and the accessories wherever they could." The audacity of the theft was compounded by the fact that club member R.H. Alexander managed Hastings Mill.

THE ROYAL VANCOUVER YACHT CLUB

By 1905 the club boasted 187 members and 43 boats, and, as the *Province* reported, was on the verge of two "epoch-marking steps." The first was a petition, to the Governor General, for a royal warrant—an honour that would make the "lusty

Bedecked in an array of sailing clothes—sweaters and blazers, caps and hats—the men of the Vancouver Yacht Club pose for a group portrait at Belcarra Park around 1904.

THE ROYAL WARRANT

By the commissioners for executing the office of Lord High Admiral of the United Kingdom of Great Britain and Ireland, etc.

Whereas, we deem it expedient that the members of the Royal Vancouver Yacht Club, being natural born or naturalised British subjects, should be permitted to wear on board their respective vessels the Blue Ensign of His Majesty's fleet, on the following conditions:

1. Every vessel belonging to the Royal Vancouver Yacht Club in order to be eligible to wear the ensign authorised by this warrant, shall have been registered as a British vessel in accordance with the Merchant Shipping Act.

2. The ensign shall not, without our authority in writing, be worn on board any vessel belonging to the Royal Vancouver Yacht Club, while such a vessel is lent, on hire or otherwise, to any person not being a member of the club, or who, being a member of the club, is not a natural born or naturalised British subject.

Given under our hands and seal of the office of the Admiralty this eighteenth day of December, 1905.
By command of their Lordships:

CHARLES C. DRURY
J.S. WYEFIELD
J.I. THOMAS
Clerks of Admiralty

The Beaver Cup

In 1908, R.H. Alexander presented the club with a trophy fashioned in part out of the timbers of one of the coast's most historic shipwrecks, the steamer *Beaver*. Presented "to induce the building of a good staunch type of boat with fair accommodation for a suitable crew on a trip that may last some days," the cup's inspiration was the sturdiness and long life of *Beaver*. Built in London in 1835 for the Hudson's Bay Company's fur-trading activities on the Northwest Coast of America, *Beaver* arrived at the mouth of the Columbia River in 1836 and spent the next fifty-two years on the waters of Puget Sound, the Inside Passage, the Fraser River and Burrard Inlet, working as a fur trader, passenger steamer, gunpowder storage hulk, Royal Navy survey ship, logging-camp supply boat and tug.

Wrecked in 1888 thanks to either a strong current or strong drink in the wheelhouse, according to different versions of the story, *Beaver* ended her days stranded at the entrance to Vancouver Harbour before slipping beneath the waves for good in 1892. Even in ignominious death on the rocks, *Beaver*'s remains were revered by locals and tourists as "the pioneer ship" of the coast. Souvenir hunters scrambled over the hulk at low tide,

hacking away at her timbers and machinery. A large number of souvenir walking canes, furniture and other items of symbolic importance—gavels and Alexander's Beaver Cup—were made from the age-stained oak of the steamer's hull, so much so that it has been suggested enough wood was salvaged and incorporated into "Beaverabilia" to build at least three *Beaver*s. The wood in the trophy is the real thing, and a reminder not only of early yachting and a cup continually contested for nearly a century but also of an early steamer of great importance to early Vancouver and British Columbia.

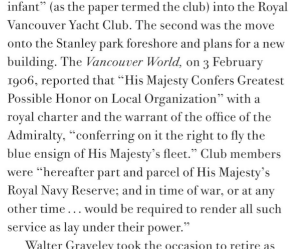

infant" (as the paper termed the club) into the Royal Vancouver Yacht Club. The second was the move onto the Stanley park foreshore and plans for a new building. The *Vancouver World,* on 3 February 1906, reported that "His Majesty Confers Greatest Possible Honor on Local Organization" with a royal charter and the warrant of the office of the Admiralty, "conferring on it the right to fly the blue ensign of His Majesty's fleet." Club members were "hereafter part and parcel of His Majesty's Royal Navy Reserve; and in time of war, or at any other time . . . would be required to render all such service as lay under their power."

Walter Graveley took the occasion to retire as commodore, nominating R.H. Alexander to succeed him. With Graveley also retired the club's original burgee, replaced by a three-colour design bearing the royal crown. In keeping with the new status of the club, plans for a new permanent building "to contain a large assembly hall with grates at each end, with provision made for small rooms upstairs and large wide verandahs encircling the whole building." This clubhouse, completed in 1908 during the term of the club's third commodore, Arthur G. Thynne, another founding member, did not last long. On 20 December 1909, a fire completely destroyed the building, along with most of the club's original records and trophies—among them the stuffed goat's head, the Mackie Trophy.

The destruction of the Mackie Trophy, albeit "somewhat mangy with age," was symbolic of the club's other crisis of 1909, when charges of fraud and unsportsmanlike conduct ended international racing between Vancouver and Seattle for several years. The bone of contention was a cup specially awarded by James Dunsmuir, the lieutenant-governor of British Columbia. The silver "cup," actually a large bowl surmounted by statuettes of Britannia and Columbia as symbols of Canada and the United States, was "to be raced for under the auspices of the Northwest International Yacht Racing Association . . . to promote yacht designing, building and racing between yacht owners of the Dominion of Canada and the United States of America." Dunsmuir presented the cup to the flag officers of the Royal Vancouver Yacht Club, who would act as trustees. While intended as an open challenge to any yacht club in the United States to race the holder of the cup, the contest for the Dunsmuir Cup quickly became a competition between Seattle and Vancouver.

Backers from both clubs built yachts specifically for the first race for the cup in 1907. The two clubs agreed that the boats would meet the international rules for the 29-foot Class, with the unspoken understanding, of course, that "God and the Devil are found in the details" and that each would have nuances of form and rig to secure a competitive advantage above and beyond good seamanship to win the race. The Seattle Yacht Club's consortium built a 26½-foot (on the waterline) yacht, *Spirit*, while the Royal Vancouver Yacht Club's consortium built a 29-foot, 1-inch long (on the waterline) yacht, *Alexandra*. The designer of *Spirit*, L.E. "Ted" Geary, "a Seattle lad just out of his teens . . . raised on the Sound . . . paddled around the water ever since he was able to walk," was already well known

Top: The large and elegant Dunsmuir Cup, also known as the Alexandra Cup, was donated by British Columbia's lieutenant-governor, James Dunsmuir, to foster international competition. The focus of a heated controversy, it has not been raced for since 1909.

Bottom: Nattily kitted out in club sweaters and caps, the crew members of *Alexandra*, headed by E.B. "Jimmy" Deane (*centre front row*), pose for a portrait in 1908.

Seattle's master boat builder
and racer Ted Geary (*front*), the
RVYC's nemesis in many a race.

Facing page: The RVYC's
Alexandra races ahead of *Spirit*
in the 1908 Dunsmuir Cup
competition on English Bay.

Vancouver Maritime Museum

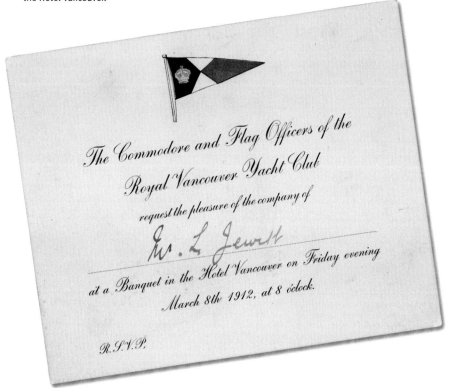

The Commodore and Flag Officers of the
Royal Vancouver Yacht Club
request the pleasure of the company of

W. L. Jewett

at a Banquet in the Hotel Vancouver on Friday evening
March 8th 1912, at 8 o'clock.

R.S.V.P.

as a self-taught, successful designer and builder. The RVYC's *Alexandra* was built in Vancouver by William Watts, scion of a famed Canadian boat-building family, from plans sent from Scotland by celebrated boat builder and yacht designer William Fyfe, Jr., whose boats raced at Cowes and for the America's Cup.

The first competition, centred around the 4 July holiday in Seattle, saw "three as pretty races as one could wish to see," according to the press. *Spirit*, skippered by Ted Geary, won the first race by three seconds. *Alexandra,* skippered by Walter Graveley, won the second race by two seconds. In the third race, *Spirit* won by a more decisive margin of three minutes, four seconds, and the cup went to the Americans. After the race, both club consortiums sold the yachts to individual members. *Alexandra* went to RVYC member E.B. "Jimmie" Deane, an enthusiastic racer.

The 1908 race, centred around Canada's 1 July holiday, was held on English Bay. Geary skippered *Spirit* for Seattle at the request of her owner, F.S. Stimson, while Deane took the helm of his *Alexandra.* Deane won the first race by a margin of 28 minutes and would have won the second race if he hadn't stopped to see if *Spirit* needed help when she ran aground on Spanish Banks, whose large sand shelf, exposed at low tide, dominated one end of the course. *Spirit*'s crew pushed off the sand and surged ahead of the startled Deane, winning by "several hundred feet" and a margin of one minute, fifty seconds. Nonplussed, Deane went on to win the third race by two minutes, forty seconds. Seattle, claiming that "the course raced over at Vancouver is not all that could be desired" and that "varying winds and strong tides played an important part" in their loss, vowed to reclaim the cup next time.

For the 1909 race, Seattle built a new yacht because Stimson had sold *Spirit* to members of the Royal Victoria Yacht Club. A consortium, headed by Scott Calhoun, turned to Ted Geary for *Spirit II,* which was launched in June 1909. Under the rules, each boat was checked by an official measurer to ensure that it was within the limits of the 29-foot Class. This was calculated not only by the length but also by the breadth and girth of the vessel, which was measured much like a pair of trousers, with the tape passing around the hull from keel to deck.

Breezy Day, by early painter
S.P. Judge (1877–1956), shows
an RVYC yawl on English Bay
around 1910.
Vancouver Maritime Museum, William and
Mary Everett Family Collection 000.089.047

Coal Harbour was the setting for much of Vancouver's early aquatic recreation. On a bright Sunday afternoon, families take to the water off the Rowing Club in the foreground, while a small cat skims along the harbour toward the RVYC club-house on the far shore.

Facing page: Gracious Edwardian boating aboard the elegant *Barney Bee,* around 1906.

When Seattle naval architect Harold Lee, the official measurer for the Northwest International Yacht Racing Association took *Spirit II*'s dimensions, he was bothered by the fact that the yacht would have been too large to fit the 29-foot rule if Geary had not carved moon-shaped scallops in the lead keel. It later transpired that Seattle's team had also sent a man into the cramped space below decks to adze out some 88 pounds of timber to lighten the vessel's stern and shift her waterline to fit into the length limits. Lee wrote to the Secretary of the NWIYRA to express his reservations. The secretary was Scott Calhoun, who in his official capacity forwarded the measurement certificate for *Spirit II* to Vancouver, as the rules required. In his capacity as a backer of *Spirit II,* however, Calhoun neglected to send Lee's letter to Vancouver.

The Royal Vancouver Yacht Club's contingent, led by Commodore C.B. MacNeill, arrived with several boats to escort *Alexandra,* with Jimmie Deane at the helm, for the competition, again centred on the 4 July holiday. Deane took the first race when *Spirit II* ran into a calm spot and could not get free. Both clubs hauled their boats for bottom work to get ready for the eagerly awaited second race, and it was then, strolling by *Spirit II,* that Deane and MacNeill spotted the irregularly "notched" keel.

The Canadians erupted with indignation. After they filed a protest with the NWIYRA, which hastily convened a meeting, the matter was settled. But then, during the second race, Harold Lee's letter was suddenly "discovered." Meanwhile, out on Puget Sound, the Americans rebounded, beating *Alexandra* in a tight race that widened into a two minute, twelve second win for *Spirit II.* With the

In her official club portrait,
Alexandra cuts through the water.

Top: *Alexandra*'s sleek lines are
evident in this half-hull model.

Bottom: The original tiller from
Alexandra was donated to the
club by Temple Wright, one of
her succession of owners, in
1955. It survives to this day as
a trophy for Frostbite dinghy
competition.

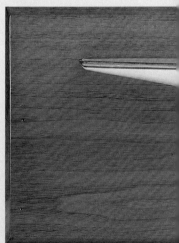

revelation that the official measurer had noted "reservations" that had not been passed on to Vancouver, and with no Canadian win in the second race, the RVYC crew was not in a happy mood when the NWIYRA (with *Spirit II* backer Calhoun sitting on the board and at the meeting) voted to continue racing. On 7 July, as the third race was about to start, Commodore MacNeill informed the Americans that there would be no race and that the Canadians were leaving—with the trophy.

Thus began a war of words. Seattle sent *Spirit II*

out on the race course by herself and, at the end of the sail, declared she had won the race, the competition and the Dunsmuir Cup. Of course, the Vancouverites were long gone. Their withdrawal "practically ended friendly relations between the Seattle and Vancouver clubs," according to the *Seattle Star.* The *Star* went on to ask Scott Calhoun his opinion of the trouble, and he fanned the flames of contention: "Rules are drafted to give a certain type of boat, and designers are paid to use their brains to get the greatest speed under the rule

SPIRIT II AND ALEXANDRA

Controversy notwithstanding, both vessels involved in the 1909 Dunsmuir Cup controversy switched nationality: each was owned by the yacht club she had once competed with, before both ended up for good in Seattle.

After the 1908 race for the cup, the RVYC raffled off *Alexandra,* and member A.J. Kapelle won her. He sold the yacht to Jimmie Deane, who had raced her against *Spirit II* in 1909 and then for years afterwards against all comers. Stripped of her lead keel during a wartime scrap drive in WWI, the beached yacht passed into the hands of Captain B.L. "Barney" Johnson of the RVYC. After Johnson, the yacht passed through the own-

ership of two other club members before the final Canadian owner, Temple Wright, sold her to Seattle in 1951.

Seattle shipyard owner Cal Blanchard seized *Spirit II* for debts left over from her construction and sold her to RVYC member Archie Selwood in 1913; he, in turn, sold her to fellow member R.A. Bindley. Bindley passed her on to Vancouver tugboat owner and club member Harold A. Jones, who rebuilt and raced her until 1947, when he built a new *Spirit* and sold *Spirit II* to Seattle Yacht Club member Webb Augustine, returning her to her birthplace.

In 1908, the sloop *Elsa May* won the 200-mile-long Texada Island race. Shown here in calm waters, quite unlike the 60-mile-an-hour winds she encountered while circling the island in a record-setting 27 hours and 8 minutes.

From the beginning, the club
was enjoyed by families. Early
member J.P. Roberts supervises
his sons on the shore from his
dry perch in the yawl *Bertha*'s
cutter, around 1913–14.

The magnificent motor-powered *Rhinegold,* built in 1911 at Vancouver Shipyard, remains in operation to this day. For sixty years, she was owned and operated by club member Col. Colin Ferrie.

RHINEGOLD

The Royal Vancouver Yacht Club's newsletter, *Motor Exhausts, Sailing Breezes,* reported on 20 July 1923:
Standing midst a heap of equipment and with salty tears streaming down his face, last Friday evening on the club float— Colin Ferrie bade good-bye forever to his old ship COLIFER— GONE but not FORGOTTEN, Sunday morning of the same week— same man—SMILES GALORE—his new purchase the RHINEGOLD under him—his crew piling aboard for a two weeks cruise.

Same weekend—a rather small gentleman, Allan DesBrisay with a catch in his breath told us of his sale of Rhinegold to Colin—a few hours, same gentleman, stripped to the waist (unable to speak) cranking HIS new purchase, a speed boat, out on the waters of English Bay—it was really a pathetic sight. "Contrasts are the lights and shadows of life."

Early club member Lew Jewett (*far left*), with friends, and his membership card from 1910.

The second clubhouse, short-lived and ill-fated, was destroyed by fire in 1909.

The third clubhouse, on the shores of Coal Harbour in Stanley Park, circa 1910.

placed before them. If the rule is faulty it should be amended, but such an exhibition of the yellow streak as was given today is inexcusable and disgusting, and will kill the sport if it is countenanced."

MacNeill and Deane fired back a response in the Vancouver and Seattle newspapers, alleging that "because a clever and ambitious Seattle boy slipped a cog somewhere in his figures . . . and a shrewd Yankee yachtsman-lawyer tried to cover it up by a characteristic Yankee trick, there is the biggest international yachting squabble on . . . that the Pacific Coast has ever known." Blasting Geary and Calhoun (particularly the latter's conflict of interest as a backer of *Spirit II* while also a supposed rule-keeper and adjudicator on the NWIYRA board), Vancouver remained adamant in its contention that the races had been ruined by "fraudulent" and "sharp tactics," and refused to relinquish the cup. Despite efforts to patch up the rift, the Dunsmuir Cup, now referred to as the Alexandra Cup, stayed in the RVYC's possession, never again to be contested. Relations between the two clubs remained strained, and for four years there was no formal contact or races. Not until 1913 and the introduction of a new trophy for international competition did Seattle and Vancouver cross swords.

The club's sailors often decorated their sweaters and blazers with individualized crests.

CHAPTER 4

RACERS, WARRIORS AND RUM RUNNERS

"If there is any particular explanation of Sir Tom's change of fortune, it may be found in the experience Vancouver yachtsmen have gained in racing against Ted Geary for the past fifteen or twenty years, so that they know most of his tricks." – VANCOUVER DAILY PROVINCE, 4 JULY 1929

IN 1913, the Royal Vancouver Yacht Club celebrated its tenth anniversary in the midst of troubled times. An economic recession gripped the region, and international tensions were high as war raged in the Balkans in a precursor to the world war that would break out in August 1914. And yet the club had cause for celebration and pride. The *Vancouver Daily Province* noted that the RVYC was "the premier yacht club of the Pacific Coast of Canada" and had "the largest fleet on the British Columbia coast or Puget Sound waters," with 140 yachts on the club roster. Three fifths of the fleet were powerboats, and yet "strongly entrenched in Vancouver harbour the sailing craft has made a strong stand against the insidious encroachment of

the motor boat in this field of sport." The "majority of the yachts are sloop rigged with yawls a good second; catboats, schooners and ketches being represented by only one or two of each of these rigs. The majority of the sailing craft are deep keel craft with outside lead ballast; what centreboard yachts there are being mainly of the Columbia River sloop type."

The growth of the club reflected a major change in Vancouver. From its working-class, entrepreneurial beginnings as a logging camp, railway terminus and speculative real-estate market, Vancouver had expanded by 1913 into a fledgling metropolis with an increasing diversity of businesses and a growing middle class. This trend

Facing page: *Turenga*'s crew poses aboard her at the Opening Day Sail Past in 1927.
City of Vancouver Archives 99-1646

The motor vessel *Andante*, built in 1911 and owned by member Alex Marshall, exemplifies the style of the club's early cruisers.

Top: John Gall's *Kingpin*, on the North Arm of the Fraser River in 1912, was an early club powerboat.

Bottom: The banner headline of the club's first newsletter demonstrated that the organization was for racers and rovers, sailors and power boaters.

continued through the 1920s and '30s. "In a bigger and wealthier Vancouver, evidence of personal success came to mean fast cars, fashionable recreation, and expensive homes." While the car was a sure status symbol, it was more easily acquired than a yacht—particularly if the yacht in question was something more than a 16-foot yawl or sloop like many of the original boats in the club's fleet.

The first two decades of the club saw the introduction of larger, more expensive, often motor-powered boats. The result, in Vancouver, as elsewhere in the world, was that "yachts served as a much surer barometer of wealth than did motor cars." That being said, not every member of the club was wealthy enough to afford a large steam yacht, or more than one vessel, though some well-off members had both sail and power vessels. For the aspiring wealthy or the working middle class, a club membership and a share or stake in a boat with other members still conveyed status, as well

as the opportunity to mingle, mix and be seen in the right circles. It was also when "the Edwardian age had come to town," as "dances, teas, receptions kept the big houses filled to the door and sparkling with lights [and] yachts glided over Coal Harbour and English Bay."

The election of B.T. Rogers as commodore in 1912 was a clear indication of these changes. Benjamin Tingley Rogers was an American entrepreneur who had followed his father into the sugar-refining business. Seeing the opportunities to manufacture and market sugar in western Canada thanks to Vancouver's links by sea to Pacific sources of sugar cane and its links by rail to markets throughout the west—and well aware that tariffs at the border kept American sugar from being much competition—Rogers decided to move to Vancouver and start up a sugar refinery.

Backed by shareholders in New York and Montreal, including his Brooklyn-based employers,

B.T. Rogers and friends at the helm of *Mow Ping*, around 1909.
City of Vancouver Archives, Bo.P.184

Rogers secured favourable shipping rates from the Canadian Pacific Railway, which was "prepared to encourage any sensible industrial project at the Vancouver terminus." He quickly won the support of Vancouver's Mayor David Oppenheimer and city council. The city agreed to purchase the land for his refinery while waiving taxes for fifteen years.

In spite of the city's bonus and the benefits of Vancouver as a port and terminal city, Rogers and his B.C. Sugar Refining Company faced a difficult start. Nonetheless, he had a guaranteed salary that began to climb, and he also began receiving bonuses that soon outstripped his salary. B.T. had a "taste for a fine lifestyle," and he indulged it with all the trappings, such as fine houses, including a two-and-a-half storey mansion, Gabriola, at Davie and Nicola Streets. Rogers also imported one of Vancouver's first motor cars in 1904, replacing it in 1905 with a Pierce Arrow that he loved to drive

as fast as he could; biographer John Schreiner recounts one incident in which Rogers was cited for driving nearly twice the speed limit, one of several infractions that "motored him into court."

Rogers further demonstrated his appetite for conspicuous consumption with his boats, including a custom-built steam yacht, the 50-foot *Mow Ping*, which cost $6,700 (many times more than the annual salary of most Vancouverites). He had joined the Vancouver Yacht Club in 1904 with *Mow Ping*, but he registered the vessel in Mrs. Rogers's name as he was an American and was not legally allowed to register, while his Canadian-born, British-subject wife could. Within a few years, he acquired a larger, more conspicuous yacht. The *Aquilo* was a 168-foot, 176-ton steel screw steamer built in Boston in 1901 for the New York Yacht Club's William C. Eno (of Eno Fruit Salts fame). Seattle steel magnate James A. Moore

Mow Ping, the first steam yacht owned by Vancouver businessman B.T. Rogers.
Vancouver Public Library

Commodore B.T. Rogers on the quarterdeck of his flagship *Aquilo*, in a watercolour portrait signed "Spy," in 1915.

Courtesy of the Rogers family

A RECEPTION ABOARD *AQUILO*

Club member Archie Selwood recalled a near-tragic race and cruise before World War I. Selwood, at the helm of *Spirit II*, which he had just bought, watched in horror as a member of his crew, Horace Stone, fell overboard while hauling in the yacht's dinghy just as Commodore B.T. Rogers's flagship *Aquilo* passed by. As Stone held on to *Spirit II*'s trailing main sheet, Selwood held his helm steady to avoid shaking off Stone. Here is the tale according to Selwood:

"Old Benny Rogers ... and his guests were gazing at us over the rail of his flagship ... which was just overtaking us ... It was blowing hard but Horace managed to inch his way along the main sheet to near our cockpit and it took four of my crew to drag him in.... After the fleet reached Clam Bay the commodore received all skippers aboard the flagship. I, as skipper of *Spirit II*, slicked up a little, and went aboard the *Aquilo* and had a couple of rums, being the centre of interest on account of Horace Stone's narrow escape, for the Stones and Rogers were great friends.

"Just when all the formalities were being rigidly observed on the deck of *Aquilo,* to my horror alongside came my dinghy bearing six disreputable, soggy, so-called yachtsmen. They got aboard anyhow, and Horace Stone saved the day by being welcomed personally by Benny Rogers himself. The other five were given a drink and taken below to look at the engines."

Top: B.T. Rogers was commodore from 1912 to 1918. His steam yacht *Aquilo* replaced his earlier yacht, *Mow Ping*.

Bottom: The Akhurst family aboard their 37-foot *I'llaway*, built in 1911.

bought the yacht from Eno in 1909 and sailed her through the Strait of Magellan in 1910. When Moore's fortunes waned in 1912, B.T. Rogers purchased *Aquilo* and brought her to Vancouver.

Rogers had just assumed the post of commodore, which he would hold for an unprecedented seven years, a term never surpassed by any successor, because of his personal profile and his exceptional yacht, which no other club on the coast could rival. He was a veritable prize of a commodore, a status symbol in his own right as well as a "a man of great wealth" who "never stinted himself on behalf of the club." Spurred on by Rogers, who "endeavoured to cultivate a spirit in keeping with the standing of a royal yacht club," the Royal Vancouver Yacht Club made a conscious effort to "enhance the standards of both racing and cruising." This meant, on Opening Day ceremonies, as the club's fleet sailed past *Aquilo* for review, "many a careless skipper was checked up for not saluting the Commodore's flag." Aboard *Aquilo,* Rogers always wore his club uniform: peaked cap, double-breasted blue blazer with twin rings on the sleeves and white trousers. And every night, he had the mate fire a ceremonial gun and lower the colours.

INTERNATIONAL COMPETITION RESUMES

After four years of cooling off after the Alexandra Cup controversy of 1909, relations between Vancouver and Seattle resumed in 1913, in competition for another international trophy. Sir Thomas Lipton, the inveterate and legendary America's Cup challenger, visited Seattle in 1912. Part of his fame was due to his habit of bestowing silver plate to yacht clubs throughout the world as he travelled, because he was such an enthusiastic yachtsman and promoter. True to form, he presented Seattle with a trophy to encourage a new competition and to end the feud with Vancouver. Racing for the Lipton Cup would be a dominant theme in the life of the two clubs for the next twenty-five years.

The competition for the Lipton Cup introduced a new type of racer, the R Class or "20-rater" boat. The R Class was one of the results of dissatisfaction with the old system of rating ostensibly similar boats for a fair race—as had happened with the Alexandra Cup fiasco. In 1905, in response to what

The Wigwam Inn, later an RVYC offshore station, was an early destination for the club's members. The club's *Kingpin* is tied up at the inn's dock in 1915.

The club's R Class boats racing
on English Bay in the 1920s.

was practically a universal complaint about rating in the yachting world, American yacht designer and builder Captain Nat Herreshoff proposed a "universal rule" that was supposed to eliminate the finagling and "clever tricks" used by designers in the past (including Herreshoff himself) to win races. Under the "universal rule," which remained the standard until 1927, the official formula for measuring and rating was applied to any size yacht; if a yacht fit within a certain size limit, she was classified according to a letter system, hence the "R." The R Class's representatives in Vancouver drew from a pool of world-renowned designers like John Alden, Charles Nicholson and Edson Shock, who drafted the plans for some of the club's most famous R Class boats: *Lady Pat, Lady Van, Patricia* and *Turenga.*

The Lipton Cup competition between Seattle and Vancouver commenced in July 1914, when two R Class yachts, built specially by each club, met on Puget Sound. B.T. Rogers sponsored the newly built *Turenga,* built from Shock's plans by Vancouver's Menchions Shipyard, to meet Seattle's brand-new *Sir Tom,* another product of the brilliant mind of Ted Geary. Ron Maitland, a member of the Vancouver contingent that had met with Seattle to set up the new competition, skippered *Turenga,* while Geary took the helm of *Sir Tom.* Seattle won the cup. The outbreak of war the next

THE JULIAN CUP

In 1906, C. Otis "Charlie" Julian presented the RVYC with a perpetual challenge cup "for yachts to be steered by ladies alone." The *Vancouver Daily Province,* in July 1913, remarked: "It might be looked upon as an important advance in the cause of equal rights for women. Mere men were still to be allowed to hoist the sails and sit around where their weight might be useful as ballast; but if they dared to touch the helm the yacht would be disqualified."

Any thought of Edwardian-style condescension is quickly dispelled by the *Province*'s account of the 1913 Julian Cup races, when a heavy squall swept through the fleet, wrecking the yacht *Britannia* and forcing other boats out of the race. "In every case the ladies showed themselves well worthy of the confidence reposed in them by the owners and crews of the racing yachts, bringing most of the yachts through in safety under most trying circumstances." The winner that year was Louise Deane, daughter of member E.B. Deane, skippering *Alexandra.*

The Julian Cup, presented to the RVYC by member Charlie Julian for the "lady skippers' race," was first won by Jessie McGeachie in 1906.

In 1915, the Imperial Tobacco Company of Canada Ltd. issued a set of forty-nine silks entitled "Yacht Pennants and Views." These silks were premiums inserted into cigarette packages.

month ended not only the competition but also all racing out of Vancouver, and it was not until 1920 that the Lipton Cup challenge resumed.

With all the competition, pomp and circumstance associated with yachting in Edwardian Vancouver, there was also another element. The years between 1910 and 1914 were also a time, according to historian Alan Morley, when "the young folk broke loose, evoking the tut-tuts of their elders. Visiting aristocrats were submerged in champagne and debutantes; there were reigning belles, and here and there emerged a new species, the playboy, like 'Afternoon Tea Charlie' Henshaw, who convulsed a yachting party and scandalized the town by providing his guests with bathing dresses straight from Paris—which disintegrated after ten minutes in the water."

AT WAR

Thanks to the wireless, Britain's declaration of war against Germany on 4 August 1914 reached Vancouver the same day. As part of the British Empire, Canada too was now at war. Crowds had gathered in anticipation of the news, while parades and other demonstrations of loyalty— including burning an effigy of the kaiser in downtown Vancouver—filled the days that followed. So, too, did preparations for war. Germany possessed a squadron of ships in the Far East that presumably could strike at British Columbia. The German East Asiatic Squadron, commanded by Admiral Maximilian Reichsgraf von Spee, consisted of two heavy cruisers, three light cruisers and a few armed merchant ships based at Tsingtao, China.

But one of von Spee's ships, the light cruiser *Leipzig,* was even closer, at Mazatlan, Mexico, standing by to protect German interests in the Mexican Civil War. And the cruiser *Nürnberg* was in the mid-Pacific after visiting San Francisco and Honolulu. With the outbreak of war, *Leipzig* departed Mazatlan and headed north. By 5 August, news of *Leipzig*'s movements reached British Columbia when a San Diego radio station intercepted a radio transmission from the German cruiser. Many feared that the cruiser was on her way to attack British Columbia, either at Esquimalt, Victoria, Vancouver—or all three.

Nürnberg might also be on her way. Only one Canadian ship, the cruiser HMCS *Rainbow,* was available to meet the potential threat.

On 4 August, a naval officer in Vancouver turned to the RVYC for help, asking for "a flotilla of fast motorboats" to patrol the seas off Esquimalt. He doubtless invoked the responsibilities of the club under the royal warrant. Royal warrant notwithstanding, the club and its commodore were ready to assist. B.T. Rogers, who had abandoned his American citizenship in 1908 to become a British subject, quickly offered *Aquilo,* which steamed to Victoria on the morning of the fifth. A dozen members of the RVYC also offered their boats, and "the club announced that a special meeting would be held for volunteers to man the flotilla." Club member W. A. Akhurst's 37-foot motorboat *I'llaway* was one of that flotilla. Her log for 6 August records she was "sailing from Vancouver on Active Service . . . On request of officials at Esquimalt the Royal Vancouver Yacht Club are sending down a number of their yachts for patrol or other work for which boats may seem best suited."

Aquilo patrolled Juan de Fuca Strait from 7 to 29 August. Her first patrol, with B.T. Rogers and an armed guard of eleven, lasted from the seventh to the ninth. On that cruise, as well as her others, *Aquilo* was not alone. The premier of British Columbia, Richard McBride, had taken matters into his own hands to augment the coast's defences. Just before the outbreak of war, he arranged to purchase two submarines then under construction in Seattle. They had been ordered by Chile for its navy, but the Chileans wanted changes made and were withholding payment. In stepped McBride with $1.2 million and a skeleton crew to motor the submarines into British Columbian waters just hours ahead of America's declaration of neutrality in the war, which would have made the sale illegal.

The subs, taken belatedly into the Royal Canadian Navy, were christened *C.C. 1* and *C.C. 2.* Canada's first submarines patrolled the Strait of Georgia, escorted at first by *Aquilo* and later by HMS *Shearwater.* With the subs was a member of the RVYC, Bernard L. "Barney" Johnson, superintendent of the province's coast pilots. Johnson, a deepwater sailor who had settled in Vancouver in 1898, had served as a coastwise master for the

"Hulme's Husky Hun Hunters," or the 62nd Overseas Battalion, commanded by RVYC member H.D. Hulme, board a troop train at Hastings Park on a wet March morning in 1916 as friends and family say good-bye. The club raised funds for a machine gun to accompany the battalion.

City of Vancouver Archives MIL.N.P.67

Top: Hastily brought to Victoria from Seattle under cover of darkness to protect British Columbia from the Imperial German Navy, *C.C. 1* and *C.C. 2* were Canada's first submarines. RVYC member (and later commodore) Barney Johnson served as first lieutenant of *C.C. 2* until 1915, when he transferred to another submarine and combat duty in the Atlantic.
Vancouver Maritime Museum

Bottom: The muddy fields and trenches of the Great War in Europe swallowed a generation of young men, including members of the Royal Vancouver Yacht Club. Here, troops unload ammunition "on the western front."
City of Vancouver Archives MIL.P.281 #34

Union Steamship Company and the Boscowitz Steamship Company. After marrying Flora Grant, the daughter of RVYC founding member Alexander Grant, he joined the club in 1904, buying his father-in-law's sloop *Siren* at the same time. With war imminent, the coast pilots loaned Johnson on a one-month's secondment to the Royal Canadian Navy as a navigator. Instead of a month, he spent five years as an officer in the Royal Canadian Naval Volunteer Reserve. Johnson served as a first lieutenant in *C.C. 2* through 1915, when he was given the job of delivery skipper for the Canadian-built submarine *H-8*. A splendid seaman and officer, Johnson performed so well that he was handed command of the vessel upon arrival in Plymouth, England, and commissioned into the Royal Naval Reserve, the beginning of a distinguished career in the submarine service. He did not return home to Vancouver until June 1919.

The threat of a German attack on British Columbia subsided when Japan entered the war as an ally of Britain's on 24 August. With no safe haven in the Pacific now that the superior forces of the Imperial Japanese Navy were against him, the outgunned von Spee headed south, fighting a British battle group and defeating them off the coast of Chile before sailing into the Atlantic and oblivion at the hands of a superior British fleet off the Falklands. With the threat of von Spee removed, British Columbia no longer needed augmented defences, and the yachts of the RVYC and their counterparts at the Royal Victoria Yacht Club were sent home.

Even as their yachts returned home, a large contingent of the Royal Vancouver Yacht Club's members went off to war to serve in the army, navy and the newly formed air corps. In all, out of two hundred members, eighty-seven shipped out. The first large group went in 1914–15 as members of the Canadian Expeditionary Force. Two club members assumed senior commands, among them Lt. Col. R.G. Edwards Leckie, commanding officer of the 72nd Seaforth Highlanders, and Lt. Col. H.D. Hulme, who took command of the 62nd Battalion. His fellow yacht club members raised the funds to buy the battalion a machine gun to help send Hulme and "Hulme's Huskies" off to war. True to traditions of the sea, the RVYC-sponsored machine gun was named "the Flying Dutchman."

The honour roll records the names of all RVYC members who served in World War I; those who were killed or died in service are specially noted.

Tom Ramsay, a member who
served both in the trenches
and at sea in WWI, returned to
racing after the war. In 1927,
he headed the syndicate that
built *Lady Van* to compete for
the Lipton Cup.

The first troops departed Vancouver on 19 August
1914, followed by thousands more. Most them did
not return home, or came back wounded, all part
of "dreadful casualty lists [that] filled long
columns in the paper day after day." In Vancouver,
"there were streets where every house had a man
overseas, and in which every block mourned its
two or three dead before the Armistice came." Of
the 3,791 Seaforth Highlanders who marched off to
the war from Vancouver, 2,515 of them became
casualties.

Sixteen of the men who marched off to war
from the comfort of Vancouver and the RVYC never
returned. Those losses included Sgt. Major Henry
Vincent Ramsay, killed at age twenty-two at Ypres.
Just before the war, Ramsay and his brother Tom
had raced in the new R Class competitions. Also
killed at Ypres was nineteen-year-old Pte. Charles
Wallen Gordon. Pte. H. A. Price, a thirty-seven-
year-old with "C" Company of the 31st Battalion of
Canadian Infantry (Alberta Regiment), was killed
on 6 November 1917.

Other club members in the army were luckier.
Clarence Wallace, a private with the 5th Battalion,
Western Cavalry, was wounded but survived. Colin
Ferrie served as an eighteen-year-old lieutenant
with the 72nd Seaforth Highlanders and lived
through the slaughter. Several members of the
club joined the Royal Flying Corps and fought in
the skies of Europe. One of them, Capt. Carleton
Main Clement, won the Croix de Guerre for his
actions over France before he was killed on 19
August 1917 at the age of twenty-one.

Other than a handful of members in the Royal
Navy Reserve, "at first there was little opportunity
for yachtsmen in naval service." That changed in
1916, when the Royal Navy began to recruit recreational boaters between the ages of twenty and
thirty-five for a motorboat patrol service in the
English Channel. After a three-and-a-half month
training period, these newly commissioned sub-
lieutenants went off to war. In all, fifty-seven young
Vancouverites, including a large contingent from
the RVYC, headed to England for training. There,
they met up with member Tom Ramsay, who, like
his brother, Harry, had fought in the trenches at
Ypres, but, unlike Harry, had survived. Allowed to
switch to the navy, Ramsay went to Greenwich to

join the motorboat course with his fellow yacht club members. The Canadians sailors were fitted quickly into Britain's local defence flotillas, a force of destroyers, trawlers, fishing boats and more than five hundred specially built motorboats, the Sea Wasps, that patrolled the waters around England and fought hard against German U-boats.

Back in Vancouver, the effects of war were felt at the club. In April 1916, the *Province* reported that the approaching yachting season "finds the membership of the Royal Vancouver Yacht Club very much scattered," with nearly half of the club off to war. "Very scanty crews remain to man the yachting fleet . . . A number of boats will not be in commission owing to the absence of owners and crews at the front . . . about the only class that promises to have a normal turnout is the small yawl class." International racing was suspended during the war, so the remaining club members kept up their competitive spirit by racing against each other and by racing model yachts, a passion that soon swept up the "juniors" of the club. The models sported the lines, rig and names of larger local and international yachts, such as *Ardrie Jr.*, *Shamrock Jr.* and *Spirit Jr.* The *Daily Province,* in December 1914, noted that "The system of construction . . . was the same as in making a half model . . . built in layers of planks to form a solid hull, which was shaped on the outside, then hollowed out with jog saw and gouge, and finally decked over. . . . These models are a work of art . . . copper fastened like a proper boat, and varnished." Racing in Coal Harbour and across English Bay on short courses, the miniature yachts stood in for their larger counterparts.

When the war ended on 11 November 1918, some of the club's veterans were already home and had been feted by Commodore Rogers at a "complimentary smoker" held on 7 February. But B.T. was not there to greet the others in November. The wartime boom had brought labour troubles to the forefront, and in April 1917, strikers on the waterfront and among Vancouver's electric streetcar drivers had been joined by Rogers's employees at B.C. Sugar. To keep the refinery operating, Rogers brought in outside workers, including some of the crew of *Aquilo,* and other men he ferried across Burrard Inlet in his yawl.

COMPLIMENTARY SMOKER

To Members of
ROYAL VANCOUVER YACHT CLUB
By COMMODORE B. T. ROGERS

"SEA WASPS ON PATROL"

On THURSDAY, FEBRUARY 7th, 1918
At The VANCOUVER CLUB at 8 p.m.

FLAG OFFICERS, 1918

Vice-Commodore
R. W. HOLLAND

Commodore
B. T. ROGERS

Rear-Commodore
J. EMERSON

On 7 February 1918, Commodore B.T. Rogers hosted a "complimentary smoker" for the club's members who had returned home from the Great War. Speeches, choruses of "Rule Britannia" and "Tipperary," "moving pictures" and recitations filled the evening. The program's cover shows a Sea Wasp on the Dover Patrol, a duty fulfilled by a number of RVYC members.

On a calm, overcast day, Coal Harbour's waters are quiet as the boats of the RVYC lie moored near the rowing and yacht clubhouses, circa 1920.
Vancouver Maritime Museum

Rogers was also in the midst of a government investigation for price fixing. Incensed, he wrote a friend that the charges and the government's publicizing the case were "most unpleasant for me— After what I did for the country when the war broke out, I think their action perfectly contemptible." He was referring to the loan of *Aquilo* to the navy. The case was ultimately dropped, but the strain of it all weighed heavily on Rogers. After a weekend cruise on *Aquilo,* B.T and his family returned to Vancouver on 17 June 1918. That night, he died of a cerebral hemorrhage.

The new commodore, F.T. Schooley, organized a reunion at the Hotel Vancouver for most of the club's surviving veterans in November 1919. Reminiscences, "rousing songs and choruses," and a recounting of the losses were part of the evening. "No such enthusiastic gathering of yachtsmen has been seen in Vancouver for many years," noted the *Province.* Among the veterans was Barney Johnson, who had just returned home to Vancouver after nearly five years of active service. Recovering from ulcers and partially collapsed lungs, he "found it hard to adjust to the abrupt transition to a peacetime life." He was not alone. It took some time for many of the veterans to return to a life they had set aside during the war, and some of them, changed by a war of "hatred and sorrow," could never return to the atmosphere of fun and entertainment that had marked the club in the years before 1914. But others could

and did, forming part of a postwar boom that saw the club and the city blossom in the "Roaring Twenties." Barney Johnson returned to the club and actively re-engaged in its activities. In 1919, he led the restoration of the club's famous old *Alexandra,* whose lead keel had been stripped off and melted down in a wartime scrap drive. Refitted under his leadership, *Alexandra* returned to the water and raced her old competitor, *Spirit,* now an RVYC boat.

AFTER THE WAR

In 1919, the club participated in a demonstration that gained it a new member and a footnote in the history books. The new member was William E. "Bill" Boeing, who had landed in Coal Harbour on 28 February and secured his new two-seater, open-cockpit, fabric-covered float plane, *B-1,* to the club's Coal Harbour dock after an hour-and-fifty-minute flight from Anacortes. Boeing, whose wartime-founded aircraft company needed to find a new market in the postwar economy, devised the flight to demonstrate how his aircraft could easily transport airmail across an international border. Using "flying boats," he hoped to convince the governments of the United States and Canada to commence a regular service (and buy more float planes) "because few cities had airports but many had waterways." While Boeing and his pilot, Eddie Hubbard, were tied up at the yacht club, Hubbard prepared for the return flight home and

Top: On 28 February 1919, the first international mail flight between Vancouver and Seattle landed at Coal Harbour and tied up at the RVYC's clubhouse. City of Vancouver Archives C.V.P.Trans. 42-43-44-45

Bottom: The 44-foot schooner yacht *Adelphi*, built for club members Claude and Wally Thicke, in 1913. She was afterwards owned by member Bert Austin. The three Thicke brothers, Claude, Wally and Herbert, were keen racers and a "fraternal team that loomed large in the early annals" of the club.

he demonstrated the plane to enthusiastic crowds. Boeing, in the meantime, made the acquaintance of club and town. He liked them both so much that he joined the Royal Vancouver Yacht Club.

When Boeing and Hubbard took off at 12:58 PM on 3 March, they taxied away from the RVYC's float, crowded with dignitaries and newfound friends. They carried a bag with sixty letters, including one from Vancouver postmaster R.G. McPherson (an RVYC member) to Seattle postmaster Edgar Battle. "When we mount upon the wings of eagles, no line of demarcation shows between Canada and the United States. May this airplane mail be the harbinger of thousands to follow." Two and half hours later, when the plane landed in Seattle, the first international airmail delivery was completed and Boeing's point was made, paving the way for many thousands—and ultimately billions—of letters to follow.

In the Lipton Cup competition of 1920, *Turenga* once again sailed for Vancouver against *Sir Tom* and lost. *Sir Tom,* clearly a superior boat, remained Seattle's favourite for years. Vancouver,

eager to secure the prize, looked for a new boat. Built by Henry Hoffar on Vancouver's Coal Harbour from Charles Nicholson's design, the new boat, *Patricia,* was named for syndicate leader Ron Maitland's daughter, Patsy, an inveterate sailor in her own right. Ted Geary and *Sir Tom* won again in 1921, though the gap narrowed, and in a follow-up race for another prize, the Isherwood Trophy, *Patricia* won for the first time against *Sir Tom.*

Maitland tried again for the Lipton Cup in 1922 and 1923, losing both times. But he did win the Pacific Coast Championship for the R Class in 1922, racing to victory in *Patricia* with Walter Thicke, Cec Gyles and M. Rowan crewing, at Newport Harbor in southern California. In 1925, Vancouver tried the Great Lakes–built R Class yacht *Riowna,* but kept the indomitable Past Commodore Maitland in command. This time it was a closer contest, but again the prize eluded Vancouver; *Riowna* challenged again in 1926 and lost. The RVYC built a new boat, an Alden-designed *Lady Pat,* for Maitland for the 1927 race, but yet again, *Sir Tom* and Geary took the cup.

The crew of the R Class sloop *Patricia*, around 1922. *Left to right:* Norman Gyles, Bill McKenzie, Ron Maitland, Walter Thicke and Nelson Clark.

INTERNATIONAL STAR CLASS

YACHT RACING ASSOCIATION

CHARTER

TO ITS

English Bay

FLEET

WITH TERRITORY AND JURISDICTION LIMITED TO THE WATERS OF—

English Bay, Vancouver Harbor and the Gulf of Georgia North of the Inter-

national boundry line — *In British Columbia, Canada.*

Know Ye All Men by These Presents

That the following individuals that constitute the

CHARTER MEMBERS OF THIS FLEET

H. E. Wylie.   H. H. Simmonds.   John Winslow.

Thomas Pattison.   R. W. Purvis.

Having affixed their signatures unto an application for Fleet Charter made by them in writing to the International Star Class Yacht Racing Association wherein they pledged themselves to organize, conduct and maintain this Fleet in accordance with, and at all times to abide by the Constitution and By-Laws of the International Star Class Yacht Racing Association and the Rulings of any of its authorized Officers or Committees and to promote interest and develop Star Class yacht racing within their territory and uphold the high standard of Corinthian sportsmanship and good fellowship that has been established by the Association and exact from all new members of their Fleet a like vow.

Now Therefore Does the International Star Class Yacht Racing Association, to the Fleet above named and within the territory heretofore described, grant this Charter, conferring upon these members and future members of this Fleet all rights, privileges and protection accorded by the Association to be by them henceforth shared equally with all other Fleets which combined form the Association.

Officially granted on this *15th* day of *November* in the year One Thousand Nine Hundred and *Twenty Two*.

By the following Officers in the name of the

INTERNATIONAL STAR CLASS YACHT RACING ASSOCIATION

Geo. A. Corry ★★★ President   *H. S. Watterson* ★★ Vice-President

G. W. Elder. ★ Secretary   *Clarence Purrington Clark* Treasurer

★ I.S.C. ★ Y.R.A. ★

The original charter, dated 15 November 1922, for the English Bay Fleet of the International Star Class Yacht Racing Association, founded by RVYC members.

Leeward Start by English Bay
Charter Star Boat sailor and
noted painter W.P. Weston
(1887–1967) shows three Stars
racing on the bay in the 1920s.

The clubhouse at Stanley Park was too small for large events. The club's first annual ball was held in 1921 at the Hotel Vancouver.

Harry Wylie (*right*), with J. Bushell aboard *Doris,* was an early and prominent booster of the International Star Class. A championship racer, he was the RVYC's first challenger at an International Star Class race, competing on Long Island Sound in 1923 and winning second place.

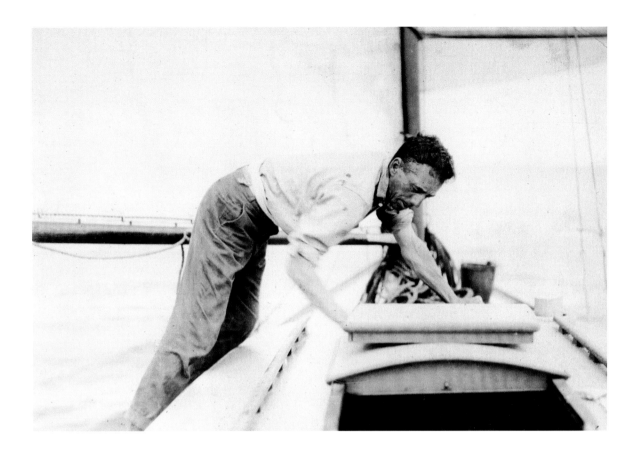

Star Class legend and champion
Reg Purves cleans up his sloop
Asthore after participating in
the PIYA Regatta at Cowichan
Bay in 1921.

At this stage, Ron Maitland and the Royal Vancouver Yacht Club were certainly sailing in the spirit of Sir Thomas Lipton, whose perennially unsuccessful challenges for the America's Cup had earned him the sobriquet "the world's best loser" for his good sportsmanship. Good sports aside, though, Vancouver wanted to win that cup, and so in 1928, a new entry, *Lady Van,* designed by British naval architects Camper and Nicholson, entered the scene. While Maitland remained with *Lady Pat,* Tom Ramsay took command of *Lady Van* for the 1928 race, which was a hard-fought win for Seattle. In 1929, *Lady Van,* this time skippered by Jack Cribb, finally wrested the Lipton Cup from *Sir Tom.* It was a particularly sweet victory, given that Geary was acknowledged as a "maestro" of yachting. There was also the matter of Geary's "clever" role in the 1909 controversy as a "rule bender." The *Vancouver Daily Province* did not miss a beat, commenting that "if there is any particular explanation of *Sir Tom*'s change of fortune, it may be found in the experience Vancouver yachtsmen have gained in racing against Ted Geary for the past fifteen or twenty years, so that they know most of his tricks."

Geary retook the cup in 1930, but "the long supremacy of Seattle ... was on the wane," and Vancouver regained it in 1931 when Jack Cribb, this time in *Lady Pat,* won. Vancouver kept the cup in 1932, in a race that featured Maitland's sixteen-year-old son Doug on the crew. The younger Maitland, like his father and sister, was a keen racer and remained active in the R Class races, ultimately commanding *Lady Pat* in the 1934 season and thereafter. Vancouver held on to the Lipton Cup thanks to *Lady Van*'s superb sailing qualities and her crews from 1935 to 1940, when another world war broke out and once again racing was suspended for the duration. By then, Maitland, Jack Cribb and the RVYC's other contenders, both winners and losers, had become club legends.

THE POWERBOATS (AND RUM RUNNERS)

The excitement and drama of racing under sail notwithstanding, the 1920s were also the heyday of the powerboat. Ironically, A.G. Ferguson, the owner of Vancouver's first steam-powered yacht, *Nagasaki,* had not joined the club. As early as 1907, regular powerboat races were taking place on the Northwest Coast, and a number of club members and their

The Canadian Pacific Railway's magnificent liner *Empress of Japan* sailed regularly from Vancouver to the Far East. When she was finally laid up and scrapped, some of her woodwork was used to build the splendid yacht *Wanderer* (*inset*).

WANDERER

The heritage yacht *Wanderer,* twice the flagship of the Royal Vancouver Yacht Club, was born out of the scrapping of another ship. *Empress of Japan,* one of the Canadian Pacific Railway's "White Empress" steamers connecting Vancouver with the Far East, operated out of Vancouver from 1891 until 1922, when she was laid up in Vancouver Harbour. The CPR sold the ship in 1924, and workers scrapped the hulk off North Vancouver in 1926. That year, using teak salvaged from the steamer, Vancouver Shipyard built the 62-foot *Wanderer* (originally christened *Cora May*) for club member T.E. "Tommy" Leigh.

In 1943, Leigh sold *Cora May* to the Department of Defence for the army to use. In 1947,

the government sold her to club member Ernie Riddell. In 1961, the boat passed to Commodore Temple H. Wright and his partner in the yacht, J.D. "Doug" Maitland, and she served as flagship for the club. In 1962, Wright sold his interest in the boat to Maitland, who renamed her *Wanderer.* In 1975, just one year shy of her fiftieth birthday, the veteran yacht again served as flagship when owner Dave Manning was commodore. Still active today, *Wanderer* survived a 1993 ramming by a B.C. Ferries vessel four times her size and is not only a reminder of early power boating on the coast but also a remnant of a historic immigrant steamer.

boats participated. Back then, a motorboat race involved minimal power (like RVYC member Knox Walkem's *Half Moon,* built in 1909 with an 18-horsepower gasoline engine) and, as a result, no extremely fast results. In the 1910 "third annual long distance cruising race" between Tacoma and Victoria, *Half Moon* won with an elapsed time of just under twenty-four hours. By 1913, three fifths of the RVYC's fleet consisted of powerboats.

The popularity of the powerboat was evident in the introduction of long-distance cruises. In 1924, Commodore Ron Maitland, "an enthusiast both in sail and power boating," led a week-long trip up the coast, deep into Jervis Inlet and the exquisite Princess Louisa Inlet. In all, eleven powerboats and seven sailing yachts, led by Maitland's power cruiser *Ysidro,* made their way up the 94-nautical mile run to Princess Louisa and moored next to

Top: Power dinghies "took others in tow" to enter Princess Louisa Inlet on the club's cruise to the fabled inlet in 1924.

Bottom: In 1924, RVYC members gather on the beach near Chatterbox Falls at the end of Princess Louisa Inlet.

INTERNATIONAL RELATIONS, RVYC STYLE

Club member Harry Bird reminisced about a Prohibition-era cruise he made to Roche Harbor on San Juan Island:

"There was a coast guard cutter tied up to the wharf, and we asked the skipper (a chief bosun's mate) what they were doing there. He came aboard and told us they were watching for rum runners ... and asked us if we had any liquor aboard. We were rather reluctant to admit that we had two bottles of Ne Plus Ultra stowed away in the bilge. The coast guard skipper seemed very pleased, however, and asked us for a drink, saying that it was a cold night and they were going out on patrol in a couple of hours.

"After a suitable celebration cementing the bonds of international friendship, I was invited to go on patrol with them. I hope I will not create any embarrassment on the diplomatic level by recalling that all we did was roar out into the middle of the strait, turned off the engine, put one man on watch and all the rest of the crew turned in for some shut-eye. I awoke in the middle of the night and heard a fast boat going by, but nobody else seemed to care, so why should I?"

The famous *Lady Van* (*centre*) races *Sir Tom* at the Pacific International Yacht Association race in 1934. *Lady Pat* is in the background.

Chatterbox Falls, which tumbled down the rocks for a few thousand feet before pouring into the sea. Extended power cruises, races and the near-equal split of trophies for sail and powerboat events demonstrated that the powerboat had more dramatically changed the tenor of the Royal Vancouver Yacht Club than any other factor since its founding, even more so than the royal warrant.

The powerboat also played another role in the years of rum-running along the coast. Prohibition, enacted in Canada in 1918, ended in 1920. In the United States, however, the enemies of strong drink prevailed, and the manufacture and sale of alcohol remained illegal until 1933. After 1920, with alcohol legal in Canada, the business of smuggling booze into the United States, by car and truck over back roads, and across the water in fast boats, became big business. A number of Vancouver fortunes were made. Joseph William Hobbs, a club member and the builder of Vancouver's Marine Building, opened a liquor-importing business and shipped crates of booze across the border in his 798-ton steel ship *Kyukuzmt,* formerly the yacht *Columbia* and one-time flagship of the New York Yacht Club.

In 1928, Hobbs converted *Kyukuzmt* back to a private yacht, and, as *Lady Stimson,* she remained in his ownership until 1929, when he sold her to W.P. Dewees, a fellow club member. Dewees renamed the yacht *Moonlight Maid,* a fitting name for an old rum-runner. Dewees was a fan of fast boats, winning the 1922 Vancouver-to-Seattle Pacific Motor Boat Race in *Reindeer,* a former U.S. Navy sub chaser that he bought as war surplus. Another war surplus purchase, the 100-foot auxiliary schooner *Naden,* bought by Joe Hobbs in 1924, became the schooner yacht (and some say rum-runner) *Mabel Dell* in 1926.

FAST TIMES

The 1920s were fast times afloat and ashore for the club. In Vancouver, as well as elsewhere in the world, this was the "golden age of yachting." The resurgence in racing, the creation of the Pacific International Yacht Racing Association in May 1920 and the booming economy lifted the Royal Vancouver Yacht Club out of the doldrums of the war years. The popularity of the sport led to an

Top: *Moonlight Maid,* Capt. Joe Hobb's famous rum-runner and an RVYC boat.
Vancouver Maritime Museum

Bottom: Some of *Moonlight Maid*'s crew posing, post-Prohibition, with bottles on deck, highlighting the yacht's rum-running reputation.
Vancouver Maritime Museum

Tamahnowus on English Bay in 1927. The 34-foot yawl, built in 1921 for Bill Templeton, was a familiar sight for two decades, winning the Beaver Cup in 1923 and twice winning the Julian Cup with "lady skippers" Mrs. E.W. Templeton in 1923 and Miss B. Pedlow in 1937.

The Jericho clubhouse under
construction in May 1927.
City of Vancouver Archives, BUP.682.N321

Royal Vancouver
Yacht Club
Smoker

January Thirteenth, 1923

Held at
The Royal Vancouver Yacht Club
Vancouver, B. C.

A program for the club's annual
smoker in 1923.

increase in the number of smaller boats—sailed for the sheer joy of it all and raced on English Bay—like the 15-foot Kitten Class dinghies, which produced some keen competition in the years immediately following World War I.

The popularity of the Kittens waned with the arrival of a new class. In 1923, the International Star Class, first built and sailed on Long Island Sound, New York, in 1911, was introduced to Vancouver and quickly caught on with its small size and fast gaff-rigged hulls. The club's newsletter, in April 1923, noted that Reg Purves "was to be seen last Sunday sailing in his new Star boat, his face wreathed in smiles—'fastest thing on the coast,' says Reg." From an initial fleet of five boats, the number of Stars grew to dominate the waters of English Bay. A few enthusiastic Star owners encouraged the club to compete in the International Star Class races on Long Island Sound. In 1923, member Harry Wylie travelled to New York with his own sails to race in a borrowed boat, his participation funded by a subscription raised by RVYC members. Wylie won second place, which inspired other Vancouverites to follow and compete far from home in Star Class racing.

As prosperity continued, the middle class swelled the club's rosters. Membership and the number of yachts (with 104 boats on the roster in 1925) increased under Commodores Henry O. Bell-Irving, G.F. Gyles, Ron Maitland, A.M. Dollar and Barney Johnson as Vancouver's population boomed from 175,000 to 246,000 in the decade. Now the middle class gained what the upper class had previously enjoyed—more leisure time—and the advent of paid vacations and national holidays created more opportunities for recreation. Not coincidentally, the growth of the Royal Vancouver Yacht Club in the 1920s was matched by the creation of other facilities, notably a series of golf courses and country clubs that sprang up around Point Grey and environs. The RVYC's nature as a less exclusive, more middle-class institution was reflected on, at the end of the decade, by member Joe Hobbs, who wrote: "Yachting in many parts of the world is considered a rich man's luxury, but in British Columbia most of the yachts are manned by the owner and a few friends, and the heavy expense of maintaining a large crew is wiped out."

Top: The Ferrie family enjoys an outing, with Colin Ferrie standing and young Jock Ferrie turning to face the camera.
Jock Ferrie Collection

Bottom: *Saxony*, built in 1911, is a beautiful and magnificent motor cruiser that also claims the honour of being one of the oldest vessels in the club's fleet.

The club's ninth commodore, George F. Gyles, shown here in 1928, served six terms: 1922–23, 1927–28 and 1940–41. With his racing family—sons Norman and Cedric, and daughter Gwynneth—he took an active role in racing and cruising for decades. His role as one of the club's "greats" was recognized with an honorary life membership in 1953.

The RVYC staff poses on the
steps of the clubhouse, with
member Stanley Brook (*top
row, wearing cap*). He served
as superintendent of the
Coal Harbour Station from
1925 to 1958.

Above: RVYC racing and cruising event program dating from 1928.

Right: The R Class boats out on English Bay in 1927. The new clubhouse at Jericho improved access for the club's sailors to the bay.

Women were also becoming more involved in the club, though none were full members, confined by the rules to an associate, nonvoting status. Nonetheless, they actively participated in the women's races for the Julian Cup and a number of other activities, as well as taking more frequently to the water as crew—in part due to the fact that, as both wages and insurance liabilities increased, members who had sailed with male employees now turned to unpaid wives, girlfriends and daughters to help them sail.

Under Commodore A.M. Dollar, the club took another step, incorporating on 14 June 1926 under the British Columbia Societies Act. The same year, the club also moved forward with plans to build a new clubhouse, this one away from Coal Harbour, which was an active industrial waterfront. In 1925, the club secured a twenty-one-year lease on 1½ acres at Jericho, close to what is now the Jericho Tennis Club on the shores of English Bay. The move from the downtown core (and beyond what were then Vancouver's city limits) was part of the development of the city in the 1920s, which included the move of the University of British Columbia from its crowded temporary quarters on Fairview Slopes to Point Grey and the construction of a loop road, Marine Drive. The owners of Star Class boats, who "always had their headquarters in English Bay," in part pushed the relocation of the clubhouse. In the spring of 1924, the Star Class skippers had built a small marine railway "at Kitsilano so their boats can be readily cleaned." The "actual move in 1927 was a great boon to the class." It was also a boon for other sailboat owners, as the Harbour Board banned sailing in Burrard Inlet, so sailboats had to be towed into English Bay, usually bucking strong tides

To build the new clubhouse, the RVYC sold debentures to members to raise $20,000. The move was not without controversy. In early 1926,

The juniors who helped the club win the Lipton Cup in 1932 with *Lady Pat. Left to right:* F.J. "Bunny" Whitcroft, J.M. "Ace" Lindsay, H.W. "Spud" Akhurst, an unidentified man and Doug Maitland.

the newsletter told the membership: "It cannot be gained without some sacrifice. This easy-going, haphazard 'getting along' must be thrown aside" because the move "will be for our future prosperity and independence." Work began in the summer; by August, "the shore works" had been completed and the site readied for construction of the building itself. Under George F. Gyles, who returned for another two-year term as commodore, the building was completed and opened in June 1927, with vessels placed there for the summer anchorage only; the original club moorings in Coal Harbour remained the winter moorage. The new clubhouse, the growing membership, the introduction of more boats, particularly the fleet of Stars and the 18-foot Flatties built for junior members—all part of the increasingly family-oriented nature of the club—were part of a decade of seemingly never-ending growth and a bright future. All of this would change, with dramatic effect, in 1929.

E.F. "Jack" Cribb was toasted by club members for skippering *Lady Van* to victory over Seattle's *Sir Tom* in 1929 to bring the Lipton Cup to Vancouver. During World War II, Cribb designed and built landing craft. He gained a measure of postwar notoriety when he converted one of his landing barges into a "palatial traveling house-boat."

CHAPTER 5

TOUGH TIMES

"Yes, the times are changed, for better or worse." –R.V.Y.C., THE CLUB NEWSLETTER, SEPTEMBER 1935

IN 1926, when the Royal Vancouver Yacht Club's members were mulling over the decision to build the new clubhouse, "Skip," the newsletter editor, reminded everyone that "The City of Vancouver is on the eve of great development. The RVYC must likewise grow and expand in a fitting manner to be worthy of this great city of ours." "Skip" was right: by 1929, Vancouver was the third-largest city in Canada. "Skyscrapers"— the multistorey Georgia Medical-Dental Building, the Hotel Georgia and the Devonshire Hotel— dominated the cityscape. And by the decade's end, three even taller buildings, the Hotel Vancouver,

the Royal Bank Building and the Marine Building (the latter built by RVYC member Joseph W. Hobbs), were all signs of the booming economy.

But by August 1929, there were disquieting indications of trouble. A recession that month was followed at the end of October by a stock market crash in New York, Toronto and Montreal. The collapse of the stock market had repercussions throughout the world, especially in Vancouver, now firmly linked to the global market thanks to its rail connections with the rest of North America and its port, which had boomed in the 1920s, with exports quadrupling between 1921 and 1929.

Facing page: The magnificent motor yacht *Fifer*'s launch at Burrard Dry Dock in North Vancouver, 11 November 1939. Designed by naval architect Robert Allan, the 100-foot *Fifer* was built for Capt. William Crawford, president of Empire Stevedoring. After wartime service as an auxiliary naval vessel hunting for Japanese submarines, *Fifer* returned to yachting. Owned at various times by R.M. Andrew, Edward Lowe, the RVYC's Clarence Wallace (who used it as his vice-regal yacht when he served as lieutenant-governor), celebrity lawyer Melvin Belli and John Manning, *Fifer* is now in private hands in California.
Vancouver Maritime Museum

Distributing food to the jobless in Vancouver at a "jungle," a camp for the homeless, at the Sunnyland City Dump, during the "hungry thirties" of the Depression.
City of Vancouver Archives Re.P.5.1 N.4.1

During the difficult years of World War I, and again during the Depression, some club members turned to the joys of racing model yachts. The tradition continues to this day. Here, a race gets underway with a rowboat assist on Lost Lagoon in Stanley Park in the 1930s.
Vancouver Maritime Museum

The plummeting of commodities prices around the world particularly hit Vancouver, which shipped wheat from the prairie provinces as well as forest products from British Columbia's logging industry. Canadian exports dropped by half between 1929 and 1933, a reflection of the economic damage the Depression wrought on Vancouver. Unemployment rose to 24 per cent, and by 1936, more than eleven thousand owners surrendered their properties to the city for failure to pay taxes. Hordes of unemployed and the homeless descended on Vancouver, "the Mecca of the unemployed," to take advantage of the warmer climate, and shantytowns sprang up on public lands. The Depression left Vancouver "more scarred than any other city in Canada."

BARNEY JOHNSON

The start of the Depression came as B.L. "Barney" Johnson ended his first year as commodore. During World War I, his submarine *H-8* had hit a submerged mine and lost its bow. He calmed his crew and resurfaced the boat. Working his way along the forward guy wire on the partially submerged deck, he found his own torpedoes sticking out of their tubes, the bow caps that protected them gone. He kept silent, and ran his damaged submarine on the surface, out of enemy waters and

home, in a harrowing voyage across the English Channel. No better man could have been at the helm of the Royal Vancouver Yacht Club when the Depression hit. The club remained in active international competition, and in 1930 Johnson initiated a new race that attracted competitors from Victoria and the United States. Known as the Swiftsure Classic, the new race started at Victoria's Cadboro Bay and ran on a 136-nautical mile course to and from the *Swiftsure* Lightship, off Cape Flattery at the entrance to Juan de Fuca Strait. No easy course, the Swiftsure was a test for the "keenest of rough-weather yachtsmen." Johnson's original idea for the race was a circumnavigation of Vancouver Island, "patterned after the Fastnet," according to Swiftsure race historians Humphrey Golby and Shirley Hewett. But "Seattle's pragmatic Ray Cooke responded somewhat cynically that they could all get just as seasick if they sailed around the *Swiftsure* Lightship in the open ocean."

Barney Johnson had just purchased the 54-foot yawl *White Wings II* from club member Walter Cline, rerigged her with a genoa jib and renamed her *Westward Ho*. The name, not coincidentally, was also the name of his favourite rum drink. He raced and lost to a Seattle boat in 1930, but won in 1931, though some of the Royal Victoria Yacht Club's entrants alleged that he had won only because he

Barney Johnson's *Westward Ho* catches the wind. His favourite cocktail was also named the "Westward Ho." He was commodore in 1929–30, 1936 and 1950.

had met the *Swiftsure* Lightship as she headed into port to be relieved. There was no Swiftsure race in 1932, but in 1933, as the economy began to slowly improve, the race was revived, and again *Westward Ho* took the prize. A Seattle yacht won in 1934, and then the race went into a hiatus brought on by the continued Depression and the war. It would not return until 1947. Johnson, meanwhile, survived the bankruptcy of one of his companies, but in June 1937, "because of hard times," he sold *Westward Ho* to a camp for teenagers on Orcas Island.

Westward Ho was not the only Depression-era sale Johnson made. In 1930, he was commodore when the club sold its Coal Harbour clubhouse to the Government of Canada for use by the Royal Canadian Naval Volunteer Reserve. The RVYC, thanks to the sale of the old clubhouse, and the fact that it did not lose many members, held on through the Depression years. In 1931, the membership stood at 176 with 108 boats—4 more boats than the 104 listed in 1925. What the numbers did not show were the members who could not afford

to hang on, among them young Bob Gibson. Gibson, filled with a love of boats, had built a 16-foot V-bottomed speedboat in a friend's garage but couldn't afford to buy an engine, so he sold it. In fact, Gibson couldn't afford the five dollars a month membership in the club, and so he had to quit.

Becalmed but Still Afloat

From 1931 to 1935, the highly regarded Eric W. Hamber was commodore. Although "few new yachts came into the club, sailing and powerboat activity was well maintained and the membership total was fairly consistent." In addition to being remembered as a keen yachtsman and an exceptional sportsman, Hamber (who served as lieutenant-governor of British Columbia from 1936 to 1941) is warmly recalled for leading the RVYC "in the difficult Depression years when economic conditions retarded normal development." His flagship *Vencedor* was a steam-powered training vessel purchased from Joe Hobbs, who lost his fortune in the construction of the Marine Building.

A model of Eric W. Hamber's steam yacht *Vencedor*. Hamber was lieutenant-governor of British Columbia and an active member of the RVYC, serving as commodore from 1931–35.

Captain B.L. "Barney" Johnson, CBE, DSO, RCN, was a larger-than-life figure. His service in both world wars, his three terms as commodore, his active role in promoting the club, his support of the juniors and his adherence to the proud traditions of the navy, all made "Old Barney" a legend in the RVYC.

Oil pastel portrait by Kathleen Shackleton, RVYC Collection

Apart from the occasional business failure and the sale of a boat, the club and its members held on through the "dirty thirties," but for some it was very difficult. When members who lost their homes moved aboard their boats, the club's anchorage at Coal Harbour became a regular community, with milk and newspaper deliveries to the floats. Lyall Bell, born in 1923, remembers the Depression years well. His father, Oliver H. Bell, was a salesman for Begg Motors and a member of the club's executive. The Bell family retained their home, boat and membership, but Lyall recalls that many bills owed to his father were paid with goods and services, not cash. A Fraser Valley farmer's radio, accepted by the elder Bell instead of a payment, became a gift to young Lyall, who helped out with paper routes, selling the *Toronto Star* and *Vancouver Province,* as well as magazines like *Maclean's.*

In April 1935, the *Motor, Air, and Boat News* reported that the RVYC fleet stood at seventy-two power yachts and fifty-four sailing yachts. "A con-siderable payroll is the result of the outfitting sea-son . . . the RVYC actually represents quite a thriving industry in the City of Vancouver." In August 1936, *Pacific Travel Monthly* reported "there are 575 members with approximately 160 yachts registered at the club." The reality behind these stories was that it was still tough going for the club and its members, and there was no extra money for new boats, new races or the expense of large crews. A number of boats sat idle, and "racing was at a low ebb." To encourage more racing, a group of club members—Roy Ginn, Reg Purves, Bill Roedde, Cedric Dill and Ron Jackson—"spent many pleasant hours arguing" over an ideal one-design racing craft that could be built "at relatively small cost and could also be used for cruising." Taking their design to local naval architect Tom Halliday, also a club member, who drew up the plans, the group then decided to hold a raffle to raise the $2,315 needed to build the first boat. The raffle, in the spring of 1935, raised $2,500 by selling five hundred $5 tickets.

Facing page: The proud crew of Eric Hamber's 150-foot steam yacht *Vencedor.*
Vancouver Maritime Museum

This page: W.A. "Bill" Roedde, an active and enthusiastic sailor, joined the club in 1905 and served overseas during World War I. After the war, he energetically resumed his membership and, during the "hungry thirties," led the group that designed the famous Roedde Class for the club.

"ROYALTY VISITS BELLINGHAM"

On 25 May 1935, Ronald Kenvyn of the *Vancouver Daily Province* reported:
When the Royal Vancouver Yacht Club was in its early days as a "royal" organization and proud of its blue ensign, there was a cruise to Bellingham. The Bellingham newspaper announced the event under the headline "Royalty Visits Bellingham." Naturally the Vancouver men threw out their chests. Charlie Julian, the secretary, had a rather ornate uniform of white with gold trimmings. He and a friend, who was also wearing yachting rig, went into a bar for a little refreshment and got into a conversation with the barkeep, a friendly soul. The friend had a festered finger, which was bandaged. The barkeep remarked, "You want to be careful of those brass instruments. You can easily get a cut poisoned." The Vancouver men looked somewhat blank, so the barkeep added: "Ain't you guys bandsmen?" Exit the pride of the RVYC!

The Eight Metre *Santa Maria* drives for the finish line at the Xth Olympic Games at Los Angeles in 1932 under skipper Jack Cribb. She won the silver medal that day.

THE RVYC GOES TO THE OLYMPICS, 1932

Yachting first appeared as a sport at the 1896 Olympic Games, though the event was cancelled due to bad weather. Yachting reappeared on the Olympic schedule in France in 1900, and then went through an eight-year hiatus before resuming in 1908. Since then, yachting (redesignated as "sailing" in 2000) has been a part of the Olympics.

In 1932, the Olympic yachting competition included the Star, Six and Eight Metre Classes. Since the games were held in Los Angeles, for the first time the Olympics were close enough to spare a great deal of expense for the RVYC (and others) to contend, especially in that Depression year. RVYC members competed in all three of the classes. Harry Wylie (skipper) and Henry Simmons raced the Vancouver-built Star Class challenger *Windor*, having won the chance to represent the club

after Wylie beat all comers at the Canadian elimination trials. Racing off San Pedro, California, *Windor* won third place, but not the Olympic bronze medal. Wylie shipped *Windor* home before he realized that he and Swedish contender Gunnar Asther had tied with exact scores. A sail-off was ordered to settle which of the two third-place winners would take home the bronze. Without *Windor*, Wylie couldn't compete, so the medal went to Asther by default.

The RVYC's Jack Cribb and crew of Ron Maitland, George Gyles, Harold Jones, P.D. Gordon, Hubert Wallace and Edward Day did better, winning a silver medal in the Eight Metre Class. And in the Six Metre Class, club members Philip Rogers, Gordon Boultbee and Ken Glass, with Gerald Wilson as skipper, won a bronze medal.

George F. Gyles's silver medal for second place in the Eight Metre Class at the Xth Olympiad in 1932.

Gerald Wilson's bronze medal for third place in the Six Metre Class competition at the Xth Olympiad in Los Angeles in 1932.

Harry Wylie's commemorative medal from his participation in the Xth Olympiad in 1932 at Los Angeles. He placed fourth in the Star Class competition.

A 1932 Olympic Games blazer crest.

Harry "Skipper" Wylie, racer and champion, "had an uncanny knack of keeping a ship moving in practically a dead calm." Here, he strikes an uncharacteristically motionless pose.

The clubhouse and dock, with members hard at work on their boats, on 6 July 1938.

Leonard Frank photo, Vancouver Public Library 15788

The night of the raffle, "due to formalities," was one of "suspense." Hal Straight, sports editor for the *Vancouver Sun,* reported: "This is a country for boats; they love boats here, and they all wanted this pretty little thing." Part of the reason the raffle was eagerly followed was that a number of members did not have the means to own a boat, so they crewed on others' yachts or were social members. As the process of attrition whittled away ticket holders, Straight noted comments such as: "My gosh, I was only one away . . . just missed it— was darned near a yachtsman." The winner was Jack Storey, who immediately jumped up and "announced Bill Roedde his skipper, because Storey knows no more about sailing than we do about malted milk shakes. But he intends to learn."

Storey named his new 30-foot sloop *Carita* and, true to his promise, had Roedde skipper her. But Storey soon sold *Carita* to Bill Roedde and Ron Jackson. Pleased with the result, Roedde and his friends decided to try and launch more of the sloops. The club's newsletter, in September 1935,

reported that Roedde "has been walking around with a pencil in his ear and an armful of plans for some time" and that the planned "one-design 30-foot sloop . . . would be a fine thing for yachting." By early 1936, the club's racing committee decided to build five more at $2,500 each, but another raffle would not work, "for the Depression was still being felt by members." So four "angels" were approached to guarantee payment to the shipyard: Col. Victor Spencer, Ken McLennan, Austin Taylor and Capt. Bill Crawford. The group named the new boats the Spencer Class in honour of Colonel Spencer. To keep up enthusiasm for the new boats, the club auctioned five miniature models of the new Spencers on 28 May 1937. The five full-sized Spencers helped revive not only racing but also some of the club's spirit in the last years of the Depression.

By 1938, some frivolity had returned to the club. "An impromptu cabaret in the festive spirit of Halloween" was followed by the annual smoker, with an evening of witty exchange and "lies."

"Harold Jones and Commander Barney Johnson might be prevailed upon to discuss each other's lack of sailing knowledge. Mr. Jones would need no encouragement to relate the story of the battle of the Spencer craft, in which he defeated the Commander in a two-boat sailing duel. Barney would also be delighted to dwell on Jonesey's shortcomings."

In fact, Harold Jones had no shortcomings, and in 1939, was elected commodore. Jones, a tugboat skipper and owner of one of the coast's largest tow-boat firms, told the *Vancouver Province* about his qualifications for the job. "I was born with a boat in my arms. In 1906 my father gave me the *Ruth,* and I paddled all over these waters with her. Then I had *Rosena K,* which I nosed into every nook and cranny along this coast. I sold her in 1917 and picked up the *Roitoiti,* which I got rid of when I went east. On my return I bought the *Artful Dodger,* and in 1924 I went into sailing, buying *Spirit II.*" The *Province* reported: "Up until the last few years Jones was the most aggressive yachtsman in the club. He skippered every race for blood. But lately he has been content to go more for the ride."

Jones's election on 19 January 1939 was at an annual meeting marked with humour. "There was talk about formal uniforms and a merry-feeling gentleman suggested that in honour of Sally Rand Week, fans should be the choice," but the thought of yachting nude with strategically placed hand-held fans in the style of the notorious dancer did not meet with approval. "Later, when the discussion was very caustic, lengthy and tiresome, this same fellow interrupted with, 'May I suggest something, Mr. Commodore?' 'Thank you. May we have a short recess for just a teeny-weeny drink?'" The *Province*'s report on the annual meeting captured some of the lighthearted spirit with a humorous cartoon of the RVYC executive clustered about on a float and a yacht. A smiling Commodore Jones, atop the mast, one hand clutching a telescope, saw "Clear sailing ahead."

The magnificent 125-foot *Taconite* was designed by Tom Halliday and built in 1930 for the Boeing family by Boeing Aircraft of Canada at its ship-yard on Coal Harbour. She is planked using Burmese teak with yellow cedar frames and has a keel of Australian gumwood. Teak was also used for the superstructure, the decks and much of the interior panelling, as well as some of the interior furnishings. Club member Gordon Levett now owns *Taconite*.
Courtesy of Gordon Levett

The RVYC's Executive Committee
was delightfully caricatured
for the *Daily Province* in 1939.

"The New Yachtsman," 1939

In May 1939, the *Daily Province*'s marine editor, Ronald Kenvyn, reported on the opening of the summer season, noting that times had changed:

I was talking to the skipper of a racing Star yacht recently and received an eye-opener as to the modern yachtsman. The present crop of Corinthians is highly scientific and to one who had sailed in the days when all you had was a boat and a suit of sails and did the best you could, these new ideas were of intense interest.

I gathered that the present-day racing skipper makes a close study of his sails. He works out the best system of placing the cloths and the curve of the sail is of the utmost importance. The flow of air against what is termed the "foil" is a matter of scientific calculation. There is talk of high wind pressure and low pressure areas.

The question of sheeting the sails is also a topic to be approached with reverence. "Sheeting," for the benefit of laymen, has no reference to bed linen but means the ropes attached to the sails for the purpose of hauling them in or easing them off. The question of strain on the sails caused by the angle of the sheets is a serious point and there are varying schools of thought.

When you learn that these modern skippers refer to their sails as their "power plants" it gives you an idea of the heights sailing has attained.

The RVYC's Coal Harbour moorage served as a floating home for some members during the difficult years of the Depression.
Vancouver Maritime Museum

WORLD WAR II

The optimism of "clear sailing ahead" did not take into account the possibility of war. The rise of fascism in Europe, initially heralded by the rise of Benito Mussolini to power in Italy, was followed by the election of Adolf Hitler as chancellor of Germany in 1933 and the quick seizure of power by the Nazis. In Asia, nationalistic and militaristic Japan launched a brutal war against China in 1937. President Franklin Roosevelt reinstituted conscription and began to arm the United States for the war he saw coming. The alliance of Germany, Italy and Japan as the Axis Powers raised the spectre of war around the globe.

At 11:00 PM on 31 August 1939, Lieutenant-Governor Eric Hamber, his wife and six guests were aboard *Vencedor* lying at anchor off Jericho near the club. The yacht's log has a simple entry: "Heard Radio. War Poland & Germany." Hitler's unprovoked attack on neighbouring Poland would inevitably draw the British Commonwealth, which had treaty ties to the beleaguered Poles, into the fight. The next day, *Vencedor*'s days as a pleasure vessel ended as the crew went off to war. The last entry in her log, made around July 1940, lists six crew members and their ranks in the army and navy. As the world again descended into conflict, yachting went into a hiatus.

Out of a total RVYC membership of approximately six hundred, more than two hundred served in the army, navy and air forces by the end of the war. Club members who were veterans of World War I, including Colin Ferrie, Barney Johnson and Tom Ramsay, quickly answered the call to arms.

Members who served in the navy—in all, 110 of them—fought close to home in the Aleutians and in the North Atlantic in the deadly battle against U-boats. A number of them served in motor gunboats (MGBs) in the English Channel and the Mediterranean, including Corny Burke, Tommy

The Rev. John Antle (*right*) had a long and distinguished career in the clergy and in the club, merging his love of God and the water with the establishment of the Columbia Coast Mission. Here, he poses aboard the motor yacht *John Antle* at London Docks in July 1933 with Maj. W. Lukin Johnston, the Vancouver correspondent for the *Times*.

City of Vancouver Archives Port.P.1295.N/679

John Antle and *Syrene's* Figurehead

The bare-breasted figurehead jutting out from the RVYC Jericho clubhouse is a reminder of a remarkable early club member, the Rev. John Antle, and his 74-foot steam yacht *Syrene*. John I. Thornycraft & Sons built her at Hampton on Thames in 1921 for a Greek owner, who named her Σειρήν (or *Seirēn*). Renamed *Syrene,* the 75-foot yacht passed into the hands of Antle, one of the original members of the RVYC, in 1933.

John Antle, born into a Newfoundland fishing and sealing family, had a lifelong love of the sea. Ordained in 1892, he served parishes in the Maritimes until the Anglican Church moved him to the west coast and eventually to Vancouver. He built a 14-foot racing dinghy, *Laverock,* in his backyard, and joined the Vancouver Yacht Club in 1903. That same year, with his nine-year-old son as crew, Antle cruised up the Inside Passage. Inspired by the arrival of the steamer *Cassiar* with four badly injured loggers from an isolated northern community, he determined to bring medical help, schooling and the Gospel to a 20,000–square mile parish of coastal logging camps and Native settlements on a route that reached from Vancouver up the Strait of Georgia and Discovery Passage to Alert Bay.

In 1905, Antle founded the Columbia Coast Mission and began sixty-five years of service to the northern coast by sea. The mission outlived him by more than two decades. After building hospitals and churches in some communities, and providing medical and religious services aboard his auxiliary schooner *Columbia* in other areas, Antle decided to add another vessel to the fleet in 1933. He journeyed to England to buy *Syrene* and, with himself at the helm and a four-man crew, sailed her to Vancouver.

Antle removed *Syrene's* bare-breasted siren figurehead because he "deemed it unsuitable for a mission boat" and presented it to the club, where it has remained on prominent display for nearly seven decades. *Syrene* remained with the Columbia Coast Mission for only five years; in 1938, after the construction of *Columbia II, Syrene* was sold. She passed through two private owners, then in 1942, the B.C. Forest Service bought *Syrene* for use up the coast—in her old waters—until they retired her in 1977. RVYC member Jerry Rendell bought *Syrene* that year, bringing the Reverend Antle's boat into the club, though figurehead and boat were never reunited.

John Antle's private yacht, a 48-foot yawl, *Reverie,* was his last home. After retiring in 1936, the seventy-one-year-old Antle bought *Reverie* in England in 1940 and sailed her through wartime waters to Vancouver with a young boy as his crew. After the war, the octogenarian Antle decided to take a cruise to the West Indies, but his health failed him, and, with help sent from the club, he returned home to live out his remaining years aboard *Reverie,* moored in Coal Harbour at the club's floats. The Rev. John Antle died aboard his boat at the age of eighty-four on 3 December 1949.

Top: *Syrene*, purchased by the Rev. John Antle for use as a mission boat, yielded its figurehead to the club. After serving the church, *Syrene* is now owned by Jerry Rendell and still on the RVYC roster.

Bottom: The fulsome figurehead of the yacht *Syrene* was removed by the Rev. John Antle and donated to the RVYC because it was too racy for a mission boat.

Ladner and Doug Maitland, whose escapades and feats earned them the nickname of "the Three Musketeers." Other members such as Ken Glass, John Leckie, Albert Morrow and Steve Rendell also served on MGBS. Ken McRae returned to Vancouver with the OBE and the rank of commander, and took command of the "stone frigate" training base HMCS *Discovery*. Bill Dolmage and Ted LePage also won the OBE. They served as wartime salvage officers and "spent much of their time on the ocean bottom" as divers. Two women, Ruth Tomlinson and Pat Wilgress, joined the Wrens.

Fifty-four members served in the army, among them Lt. Col. John W. Toogood of the British Columbia Regiment. One club member, J.V. "Jack" Christensen, spent the war in harrowing circumstances as a prisoner of war in Hong Kong and Japan.

Fifty men from the club also served in the air force, among them World War I veteran K.G. Nairn, who ended the war as an air vice-marshal, while Squadron Leader R.W.R. "Bob" Day fought the Japanese in the skies over Burma. Three women—Catherine Day, Marion Downs and K. Schwengers—also joined the air force. Eleven men served in the merchant marine, while another two women joined the Red Cross.

The horrendously high ratio of casualties among the club's ranks in World War I was not repeated; losses in World War II were limited to fifteen killed. Navy men lost included Lt. Armour Bull, Eric Ditmars, David Killam, Lt. Stuart C. Lane, and Lt. Fred Whitehead. Among those lost in the air force were Flight Lt. William John "Bill" Maitland, Flight Sgts. Gerald Bartle and George Walkem, Leading Aircraftman Robert Johnston and Pilot Officer Edwin Bullen. There were two army casualties, Capt. Robert Rankin and Pte. Robert Hume.

THE VOLUNTEER YACHT PATROL

On 25 April 1942, the *Daily Province* reported, "Cruising and sailing activities of the club have been all but cancelled due to wartime restrictions and members on active service. However, the club, which started some 39 years ago with a handful of members and 13 boats, will probably emerge bigger than ever when the war is over." Although the club's regular activities were suspended, some

The Seaforth Highlanders, including the RVYC's Col. Colin Ferrie, head off to fight overseas.
Jock Ferrie Collection

members were actively engaged on the home front as a Volunteer Yacht Patrol from 1940 to 1944. With the outbreak of war in September 1939, Commodore Harold Jones wrote the government to report that "as a Naval Reserve Club and the holder of a warrant to fly the Blue Ensign," the RVYC "wished to tender the services of either the club as a whole or any individual members."

The government suggested that the names of individual members be sent to the "Admiral Commanding Reserves, London" in a month. Chafing at waiting, some of the club's members "felt that their past experience and present circumstances demanded that they lend their efforts to assist in some way." The idea that they came up with was to form a Volunteer Yacht Patrol "to be used in case of emergency," much like the land-based Civilian Protection Committee.

On their own initiative, a group of club members resolved in July 1940 to "form ourselves into a unit and request naval instruction to fit ourselves to be of value to the local authorities." Barney Johnson, already appointed Naval Officer-in-Charge for Vancouver, was also at the meeting. He suggested that the unit only have twenty-five members, with five boats, and that he would provide naval officers to train them. They wouldn't be official, but they would be a great help.

Training began on 20 August, starting with a series of lectures on navigation, signalling, and seamanship, and with runs on their boats two nights a week. The same day, the government

Doug Maitland's *MGB 657* in the Mediterranean during World War II.
Paddy Thomson

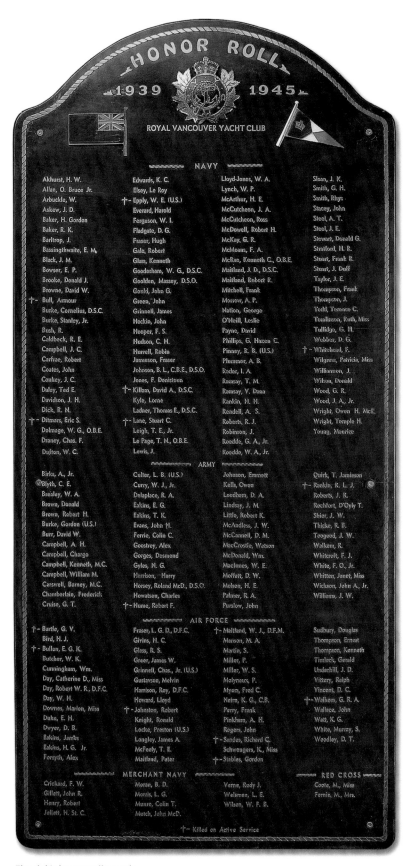

The club's honour roll records the names of those who served—and those who made the ultimate sacrifice—during World War II.

issued a call for volunteers for active service in the Royal Canadian Navy. Five members of the club's new "naval training section" were immediately accepted for duty. As the war continued, more members of the section, which quickly became the Volunteer Yacht Patrol, were also accepted for duty. In all, sixty-five members of the club passed through the naval training section to become members of the navy.

In September 1941, the patrol, at Barney's suggestion, charted local waters. The casual attitude of the government toward the Volunteer Yacht Patrol and its unofficial status changed with the Japanese attack on Pearl Harbor on 7 December 1941. Japan's attack on the British colonies of Hong Kong and Singapore at the same time suddenly thrust Canada into a new conflict with an enemy whose navy could strike the west coast. As well, the declaration of war with Japan on 8 December alarmed local and military officials, who saw British Columbia's Japanese and Japanese-Canadian population as a potential threat.

Acting on the navy's instructions, the RVYC's Volunteer Yacht Patrol mobilized on 9 December to "assist in immobilizing the local Japanese fishing fleet." For the next ten days, the patrol, working with naval officers, helped round up 1,182 fishing boats from the Fraser River and Burrard Inlet. This was the first step in what became a large-scale confiscation of property, incarceration, and, finally, the removal of the Japanese-Canadian population without regard for their citizenship, their loyalty, the impact of these actions, or their rights. Fear of Japanese espionage and sabotage, patriotism and racism all played a strong role in the government's decision, which today is viewed as an overreaction.

The roundup of the fishboats, which included "dismantling" their engines, concluded with an official note of thanks from the Naval Secretary in Ottawa. "The Department is extremely grateful for the valuable service you have rendered, and the efficiency and willingness with which you carried this out is much appreciated." The appreciation of the navy extended to a new assignment—a blackout patrol of Burrard Inlet that began in 1942 and lasted to the end of 1943, when, in the face of the Japanese defeat at Midway and the Aleutians,

"The Three Musketeers"

The RVYC's most famous warriors of World War II were three friends—Cornelius "Corny" Burke, Thomas Ellis "Tommy" Ladner, and John Douglas "Doug" Maitland—who joined the navy and fought alongside each other in motor gunboats (MGBS) in the same flotilla for the entire war. One of Corny Burke's former crew members, L.C. "Rover" Reynolds, described them as "a trio of fascinating contrasts and yet they were in many ways complementary to another. Maitland, the senior, was outwardly hard-bitten and crisp of speech; Corny was rugged, forceful and decisive in all his actions; and Ladner possessed a penetrating brain, a serious nature and a far more sensitive personality. They had enormous zest for life and refreshing ability to throw off the weight of responsibility and to relax light-heartedly off duty, when their sense of humour was rarely dormant."

After the three Vancouver yachtsmen became naval officers and learned how to fight in the waters of the English Channel and the North Sea against German E-boats, they were sent to the Mediterranean in 1943. On their way to Gibraltar in a convoy of boats, a German U-boat surfaced and strafed Maitland's boat, *MGB 657,* setting one of his spare fuel tanks on fire. Maitland pushed his throttles full ahead, turned sharply and buried *657*'s bow in the waves. The water cascaded over the decks, put out the fire and *657* got away. In the Mediterranean and the Adriatic, the three, as members of Coastal Forces, participated in a number of actions that won them acclaim and decorations, including the complete destruction of a German convoy in a seven-hour running battle and the wiping out of a German garrison on an island. As they departed, Burke noticed that a German signalman on the mainland was desperately trying to get the attention of the now dead garrison. Picking up his signal lamp, Burke spelled out, "H-E-I-L," paused, and then clicked out "C-H-U-R-C-H-I-L-L" before speeding off.

For their service, "the Three Musketeers" were each awarded the Distinguished Service Cross, with bars (which means more than once—Maitland received one bar, and Burke and Ladner received two bars). All three were mentioned in dispatches "for courage, determination and skill," for "outstanding leadership courage and skill," and for "skill and bravery." The French awarded Maitland the Croix de Guerre (avec Palme) for exceptional services in co-operation with French forces in the recapture of the island of Elba.

At war's end, the three friends, whose élan and esprit de corps remain legendary among their fellow veterans and the members of the Royal Vancouver Yacht Club, returned home to resume their lives—Burke in the towing and later the travel industry, Maitland in the family insurance business, and Ladner as a lawyer—and all of them as members of the club, where Maitland ultimately followed in his father's footsteps as commodore in 1955.

The RVYC's wartime "three musketeers" on a London Street in 1945. *Left to right:* Tom Ladner, Doug Maitland and "Corny" Burke.
National Archives of Canada pa-180065

Harold A. Jones, a "capable, if exacting and dominant skipper," was commodore in 1939 and 1944–47. He is holding the Port Townsend Trophy won by his *Spirit II* in 1940.

authorities realized that the threat of attack, either from sea or from the air, was gone.

In February 1944, Rear Admiral V.G. Brodeur, RCN, Commanding Officer for the Pacific Coast, wrote to the club to thank the Volunteer Yacht Patrol and to report that since "the Defence Category for the West Coast has now been greatly reduced," its services were no longer required. "It has been noted that, since the inception of this organization, the members of the patrol have carried out their duties in a keen and efficient manner, and at all times have been available at short notice, and I wish to express the appreciation and thanks of the Naval Service for the valuable services performed by your organization." The Naval Officer-in-Charge, Vancouver, added his thanks: "It is fully realized that the time and energy expended by the various members of the Vancouver Volunteer Yacht Patrol, to say nothing of the physical discomforts experienced, have been a considerable imposition. The efforts of the Yacht Patrol have measurably reduced the commitments of the Royal Canadian Navy in this area during a period in which it would have been difficult to maintain a similar Naval Patrol."

During the war years, except for the Volunteer Yacht Patrol, the club was not active on the water. With a third of the membership off fighting, the club kept them on the rolls with a "dues holiday" for the duration of the war. Consequently, finances were tight. In January 1940, as Commodore George F. Gyles took office, treasurer Frank Wilgress reported that "if the club were to continue operations during the coming year, as it did last year, that new members would have to be brought to the club" and that "the club might have to raise the ante for mooring fees." The club's finances were so low that in April it surrendered its lease to half of the property on which the clubhouse sat (now Hastings Park), because it could not meet the lease payments, sending in $25 to cover "arrears of rentals" with the abandonment of the lease. The next three years were "caretaker" years for Commodores Gyles, J.A. Longley and J.S. "Jack" Halse. "Sailing activities were at a minimum and power boating practically nonexistent due to gasoline rationing."

The RVYC's Women's Naval Auxiliary met at the clubhouse and did their part on the home front. In March 1940, "astounding reports of progress" reached the papers. "Mrs. Gordon Farrell reported that 633 knitted garments had been completed" in the last three months for troops abroad, and "Mrs. R.E. Stanfield reported that the ways and means committee had raised over $850 in the same period." No small sum, the funds for the war effort had come from a concert, a theatrical production, "individual bridge parties" and "talent boxes." The Women's Naval Auxiliary amalgamated with other women's organizations doing war work in early 1943, its members continuing to work on behalf of Canadians serving in the navy until the end of the war.

A partial return to normalcy came in 1944, during the tenure of returning Commodore Harold A. Jones, who stayed in office for the next three years. Jones, a kind and generous man who was very supportive of junior club members, was president of the Vancouver Tug Boat Company. In 1970, the club's members of the time, many of whom had been juniors during Jones's tenure as commodore, recalled "fond memories of the 'luscious pies' handed out to them as hungry youngsters by Harold's tugboat cooks, as they cadged a ride, hitched to log booms, when becalmed along the coast."

During Jones's first year as returning commodore in 1945, the club held its first Annual Children's Day and Family Weekend Cruise. It was organized by Oliver "Olly" Bell, who was director and property manager for the Anglican Church's Camp Artaban on Gambier Island in Howe Sound, and he selected Long Bay on Gambier as the destination, beginning a tradition that would continue for decades. Christmas of 1945, the first holiday celebrated after six years of war, was marked by hopes for peace, for the return home of family and friends from the distant theatres of conflict, and for the club's return to normal. But difficult times still lay ahead.

CHAPTER 6

POSTWAR YEARS

"As the results come in, year after year, the truth becomes more and more apparent; it takes a special kind of sailor to win a Swiftsure." —HUMPHREY GOLBY AND SHIRLEY HEWETT, *SWIFTSURE: THE FIRST FIFTY YEARS*

WHEN MORE THAN two hundred members of the Royal Vancouver Yacht Club went off to war, they were granted a "dues holiday" and remained on the membership rolls, with devastating results to the club's coffers. Any thoughts of a resurgent membership and better finances, however, were not realized in the immediate postwar years. Many veterans turned to other pursuits—school, careers and marriage—and did not rejoin the club.

Some new members did join, however. J.V. "Jack" Christensen, liberated from his wartime slavery as a POW in Japan, was en route to the United States along with some sixty other Commonwealth troops when the Americans discovered their mistake and landed the group in Victoria in October 1945. Fortunately for Christensen, the East Asiatic Company's local agent helped him slip out of the holding camp, and he made his way to Vancouver and the company's offices. Convinced to stay by the Vancouver office manager, Christensen had to sail to England to formally muster out of the army, and he returned in June 1946 to Vancouver. There, the East Asiatic's Vancouver agent, Capt. Barney Johnson, also back from wartime service and ever the enthusiastic booster of the RVYC, convinced Christensen to join the club. As a veteran, Christensen was able to join for half price, which was then $75 as the club was "short of members." He crewed for years with Johnson before buying his own boat, the exquisitely turned out wooden *Neptune,* custom built and shipped out from Denmark in 1961.

The postwar years also saw a continuation of the club's shift in emphasis to the family and, in particular, children. It was necessary, because

Facing page: The Strait of Georgia is a magnificent and at times challenging sailing ground—as it has been for the RVYC's sailors for many years. This photo is from the late 1950s.

This page: The Jericho clubhouse in the 1950s.

The Bird boats were a small but significant newcomer in the postwar period. Designed by Halifax's William J. Roue, naval architect of the famous *Bluenose,* the 47-foot sloops were built in Nova Scotia. Four of the first five were imported by J.C. McPherson and W.H. Smith by railcar to Vancouver in 1946. *Swallow* was not raced, but *Buccaneer* (ex-*Albatross*), *Hawk* and *Blue Heron* actively competed over the next decade and beyond. Very good in light airs, they enabled RVYC racers to compete well against the Seattle Yacht Club.

Vancouver, despite the construction of new high rises and the availability of more jobs, was undergoing a fundamental change as the surrounding region blossomed, drawing away businesses and people. Vancouver's population grew by only 21 per cent in the 1950s, while the suburban area's population increased by a tremendous 87 per cent. To maintain membership numbers, the RVYC had to serve the needs of those who now had families to raise and some distance to travel to reach the clubhouse.

Those members who remained, as well as those who joined or, like Bob Gibson, rejoined the club's ranks (as he did in 1950)—did so because boats were their life. Gibson did not have a great deal of money, but whatever extra income he had, he poured into his boat and boating. It was the only recreation and holiday activity his family knew. "Every weekend we were out on the water," he recalls today, and his children, like those of many other members, "grew up on the water. We're a boating family." The club's newsletter, the *Seabreeze*, highlighted this new era in November 1951, advertising "family night dinners" on Sundays: "Supper for the children at 5:30 PM followed by a one hour children's moving picture show (cartoons, Mickey Mouse, Donald Duck etc.) while the parents have dinner."

One way to attract and keep families in the club was the juniors program. While junior members had been part of the club since the early days, they were, in the spirit of the times, "seen and not heard," and were not always welcome in the adult atmosphere of the clubhouse. Sandwiches and cold drinks were dispensed to them at the kitchen's back door, and teaching them to sail or navigate a powerboat was left to their parents or older siblings. In the postwar years, the club's executive began to place more emphasis on the juniors, with a watchful eye on the "baby boom" and the realization that the unprecedented number of children would swell the club's ranks in the future. Indeed, many of the club's leaders came out of the ranks of the juniors, with three future commodores—Doug Maitland, Ken Glass and Stan Davies—first serving as junior commodores.

In his third term as commodore in 1950, Barney Johnson spearheaded a move to construct a junior

The Junior Training Program, begun in the 1950s, has remained an integral part of RVYC activities ever since, and a number of the club's current members are a product of this high standard of training.

clubhouse on the wharf at Jericho. "There was resistance to spending the $15,000 required, as club funds were at a low ebb and the money would have to be borrowed from the bank. Our banker took a very dim view of our financial position, and while members approved making the loan, the bank didn't. Finally, both Commodore Johnson and Honorary Treasurer Harry Bird signed personal notes guaranteeing the obligation." The construction of the Junior Room on the Jericho Wharf was completed in 1951. The commitment to the juniors and the expenditures were exceptional, given the club's financial position. In 1952, Commodore W. Clarke Gibson worked hard to increase the cash flow, particularly by improving the dining room so that more members would eat at the club. Times were so tight that the butcher who sold the dining room its meat would not honour the club's credit, so Gibson extended his own credit to the club and paid for the roast beef out of his own pocket for a dinner party he was hosting.

In 1953, Commodore Ken Glass gave the juniors "the ear of the senior executive" by appointing Elmer J. Palmer to be honorary junior commodore.

The next step, in 1956, was the approval to spend $3,000 and begin the Junior Training Program, which within a few years blossomed to the point that Elmer Palmer, commodore in 1957 and 1958, "donated a fine enlarged landing float" to the dock in front of the clubhouse, which was "overtaxed, largely due to the increasing participation in sailing events by the junior membership." The club's accommodation of the juniors was a success. In 1957, a description of the club noted: "There is an active program of junior training ... during the summer months. This year 91 juniors took the course and qualified in seamanship in the various grades. Total junior membership in the club is now around 200." University of British Columbia physical education students organized the program, taught by two of the club's young junior sailors, Steve Tupper and Bill Falcus.

An article in the *Vancouver Sun,* in August 1957, called the Junior Training Program "Vancouver's saltiest school." The club held classes four days a week, from ten to four, at which sixty-five boys and girls, ages eight to twelve, learned "sailing, knots and splices, water safety and swimming, rowing and

Facing page: The postwar years were a time when family memberships increased and a surge in boating popularity swelled the club's rosters. Elmer Palmer (commodore in 1957 and 1958) poses with family and friends on board his sloop *Gometra.*

This page: The Pacific International Yachting Association (PIYA) Regattas, like this one in the 1950s, were a time for renewed friendly international competition.

Out on the water, the club's
famous *Urry Maru,* or starting
barge, floats in the days before
the breakwater was built.

small boat handling.... Youngsters who couldn't tie their shoes are now tying the bowline, anchor bend, reef knot and many others as well as turning out neat and strong splices.... The youngsters think it's tops, many of them being unwilling to leave the school and go off with their families on vacation." The training paid off in a number of talented sailors who won acclaim and trophies for their achievements on the water both as juniors and as adults.

CUTTING LOOSE

The postwar years also saw the antics of several colourful members whose actions were in contrast to the club's more traditional image. There was, for example, the member who took advantage of a Christmas snowfall to try and ski off the Jericho clubhouse's roof, with painful results. Then there were George Cran Jr. and Robbie Brown. On a club cruise, they arrived at Yellow Point "after some light drinking on their sloop *Hi Ho,* both sitting high up on the spreaders, no one at the helm." They zigzagged at full throttle through the crowded fleet at anchor, narrowly missing boats. Each skipper thought he was about to be rammed, hastily throwing out bumpers to soften the blow. At the last moment, Cran or Brown would lean, either to

Art and Ernestine Jefferd, honorary life members and keepers of the *Urry Maru.*

THE MASTERS OF THE *URRY MARU*

Until the early 1960s, the Royal Vancouver Yacht Club did not have a sailing secretary or any paid staff to help run races or regattas. Volunteer members, the fleet captain and the honorary hydrographer—a job "so onerous that he was accorded a position on the executive"—ran the races. From the club's archives comes a tale of those races held from 1940 to 1970, related by Jack Balmer:

"The most famous of our hydrographers was Art Jefferd, who for twenty-one years (1940 through to the end of 1960) braved the elements, summer and winter, to fire the guns at the exact time, take the finishing times, then correct the results for ratings. Art also takes the prize for being the person sitting on the Executive Committee for the longest time. Doug and Wavell Urry, professional engineers (who designed the original Coal Harbour dock and built the cutter *Cresset*), designed and built a proper starting tower on a float in 1932, when Doug was honorary measurer. It was quickly nicknamed the *Urry Maru* and served as our starting platform until the Jericho breakwater was built. Helping Art Jefferd for most of his time on the *Urry Maru* was his wife, Ernestine, a racing sailor in her own right. In their later years, these two were assisted most capably by Ernie Earle.

"Life on the *Urry Maru* was eased by a shore boat from the Jericho clubhouse, bringing lunch and tea to the stalwart committee members (on proper silver trays, no less). Nonetheless, flags were raised at the correct time, guns fired exactly when they should be, and very few protests were ever made against the Race Committee. But life aboard a committee boat is not always easy. There is a story about a shotgun misfiring its blank load into someone's foot, and I can remember the time when, in a Coal Harbour Evening Series race, Ernie Earle was starting us from a small outboard skiff. On a close reach coming into the starting line, I, at the helm of *Fulmar,* hardened up to push up the weather boats. They all responded except *Hawk,* skippered by Ralph Farris, who had no room left. The long narrow bow of *Hawk* sailed over the stern of the committee boat, leaving Ernie half awash in the skiff. The *Hawk* was, not surprisingly, disqualified.

"Other honorary hydrographers, before the office was discontinued in 1970, included Gerry Palmer, Bonar Davis, John Long, Steve Tupper, Dave Miller and Doug Day. The *Urry Maru,* after thirty-two years of service, was finally dismantled for scrap."

Harold A. Jones drives *Spirit,*
his new Ed Monk-designed
boat, built in 1946, in a PIYA
Regatta. He was commodore in
1939 and 1944–47.

port or starboard, and their boat would veer off, aiming for another vessel. They finally anchored and fell asleep. Unfortunately, they had anchored too close to the rocky shore on a falling tide. In the morning, Cran awoke first to find the boat was not rolling with the swell. *Hi Ho* was balanced perfectly with her keel against a large rock. As Cran rolled out of his berth, the balance shifted and the boat fell heavily on its side, landing on the only strip of sand within hundreds of yards.

Another adventure, this time in the Jericho clubhouse, saw the late-night rescue of Ace Lindsay after a fine meal and libations motivated him to squeeze into the dumb waiter and try to ride it down into the kitchen to congratulate the

chef. And John Yuill, who worked as a real estate agent on the coast from his powerboat *Lickety Split,* water skied non-stop behind a speedboat, all the way across the Strait of Georgia from the Gulf Islands to the Jericho clubhouse—an incredible feat on a choppy waterway regularly navigated by tugs, barges, ferries and freighters.

There were other bold members. Ken Watt, who was fleet captain in the mid-1970s, tried without success to promote the Bat Race during his tenure. The idea was to be as blind as a bat, racing around the harbour buoys at night in total darkness. As Past Commodore John Long remembers, "He held three of these crash and burn races, only to have them declared illegal. Local towboat

The race committee observes the 1958 PIYA Regatta. *Left to right:* H.J. Bird, Commodore E.J. Palmer, Past Commodore K.G. Glass, PIYA Past Honorable Secretary W.H. Day, Past Commodore J.A. Longley, A.H. Jefferd and E.S. Earle. The shotgun on Bird's lap was a signal gun and not intended to influence the outcome of the race.

operators complained to the Vancouver Harbour authorities." Then there was Charlie Bayne, who worked as "a local salesman for men's and women's swim costumes." He enjoyed a recurrent gag at the Swiftsure race each year. Hitching a ride in a dinghy to current-and-tide washed Race Rocks, Bayne would stand on a just awash rock and wait for the racers to pass close by so that he could wave at them, looking as if he were walking on water. The joke went on for years, until "On one occasion they forgot to fetch Charlie off the rock and he was nearly washed away with the 6-knot current" before someone remembered him.

SAILBOAT RACING TAKES OFF

In November 1957, a description of the RVYC stressed that "the prime interest of the yacht club is to foster the art of sailing and seamanship." In addition to initiating the Junior Training Program, the club had resumed racing with vigour. The next few decades witnessed a phenomenal growth in the variety and number of races that the club either sponsored or participated in, races that, in time, extended well beyond home shores. Racing Star Class boats resumed in the late 1940s. Those years also saw the return to competition of two of the club's great racers of the 1930s, Phil and Sid Miller. Another veteran racer of the '30s, Bill Roedde, working again with naval architect Tom Halliday and fellow club members Bert Tupper and Jack Williamson, designed a new 34-foot sloop as an improvement to the Spencer Class that Roedde had championed during the Depression. The first of the new boats, known appropriately enough as the Roedde Class, was his own *Carita II,* launched in 1949.

The postwar years introduced a number of new boats to the club. Foreign-built yachts, some with unique histories, like the "gold ship" *Gometra,* a British yacht abandoned in Norway at the start of World War II and then used to smuggle the nation's gold reserve out of the country after the

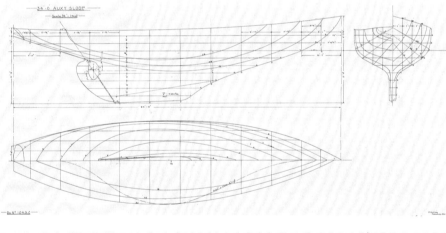

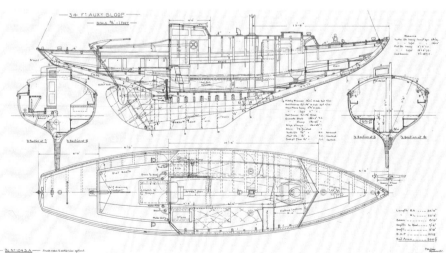

Tom Halliday's 1945 drawings for the postwar Roedde boats. The first of the Roedde Class, *Carita II*, was built in 1949 for Bill Roedde at Taylor's Boat Works.

Nazi invasion, ended up in Vancouver. It served twice as the RVYC flagship under Commodores Ken Glass and Elmer Palmer. Other imports included Dragon and Soling Class boats. The Norwegian-designed Dragons and Solings, like the Six and Eight Metre boats, were exceptional day racers that gained Olympic status and international popularity. The introduction of these classes to Vancouver signalled the club's increasingly serious approach to sail training and racing. The first Dragon, brought to the club in 1951 by W.H. "Bud"

Day, came just three years after the Dragons were selected as an Olympic class. By 1966, nine Dragons in the club were actively racing, with international competition for the Duke of Edinburgh Trophy of the Canadian International Dragon Council growing in popularity as the RVYC's sailors won regularly. The number of Solings in the club blossomed after 1969, with twelve of them as the "Pacific Soling Fleet." One of the Soling pioneers at the club was skipper Robert G. "Bob" Brodie, who would later become commodore.

Springtime at Coal Harbour in 1950. Bill Roedde "assists" from the dock as boats are cleaned of the winter's grime.
Art Jones & Company photo, RVYC

The seriousness with which sailboat racing took hold after the war was evident in the development of the Frostbiters in 1950. Year-round sailing, impossible at other Canadian yacht clubs because of harsh winters (and ice-locked lakes), was always possible, if not comfortable, in temperate, ice-free Vancouver Harbour. But starting in 1950, the Frostbiters began winter sailing out of the club's Coal Harbour station, noting that while "everyone talks about the weather . . . only Frostbiters do something about it. They get out and enjoy it. No amount of hail, rain, sleet or snow seems to deter the Frostbiter from the exhilaration of winter dinghy sailing."

The Frostbiters, pushed by members Bob Day, Ace Lindsay and Bunny Whitcroft, started with homemade plywood Sabots, but as Bill Killam notes, "Great enthusiasm in the early stages was dampened as it was discovered that any 8-foot

dinghy in 30°F temperatures and a mixture of rain and snow with a 2-foot chop from a 15-knot S.E. wind was very uncomfortable for a 200-pound man." Member Hamish Davidson, who had built laminated skis and Mosquito bomber parts during the war, saved the day by designing small 9-foot dinghies, with a centreboard, rudder, mast and sail, that, Killam explains, reduced "the discomfort of sailing in heavy weather . . . to an acceptable level." With the new D9 dinghies, the Frostbiters became a tradition that expanded to the West Vancouver Yacht Club and the Royal Victoria Yacht Club. The junior members also participated, though Steve Tupper remembers that he and his fellow juniors "sailed Sabots because senior members would not let us sail D9s."

The RVYC Frostbiters held a New Year's regatta at Coal Harbour and Jericho, matched by a regatta held on Boxing Day at the West Vancouver Yacht

The Frostbiters at the Intercity Frostbite Championships on Cadboro Bay in March 1964.
James McVie photo, RVYC

A "spinnaker parade" of Dragon
Class boats led by *Lady Nan.*
James McVie photo, RVYC

Capt. B.L. "Barney" Johnson,
warrior and racer, always had
time for the club's juniors. Here
he works with Roy Harrison
around 1955.

Club. The windup was a regatta held at Cadboro Bay each March, hosted by the Royal Victoria Yacht Club. Ace Lindsay and Bunny Whitcroft, according to Bill Killam, were responsible for adding colour to these regattas, with special themes, such as arriving costumed as tramps, retaining their outfits for the formal dinner dance hosted by Royal Vic, "at which ungentlemanly conduct was claimed by our hosts." This led to the theme for the next year, "gentlemen," which meant the Frostbiters sailed in tails and top hats, followed another year by red flannel nightshirts. Bill Killam also allows that "Cadboro Bay inhabitants will never forget the time the RVYC contingent arrived on one of Ace's tugs with a 100-watt PA system blaring out the calypso song 'Mary Ann' non-stop, day and night, from the time of arrival to departure. The pastor of the Cadboro Bay Anglican Church apologized to his congregation because he could not compete with 'Mary Ann.' The following year, the 'gang' was met on arrival by the RCMP, and an agreement was reached to the effect that 'Mary Ann' would not be played during church services on Sunday morning."

After a hiatus during the Depression and war years, the Swiftsure resumed in 1947. That year, the RVYC's flagship, the 66-foot sloop *Spirit,* belonging to Commodore Harold Jones, competed. In 1952, the club sent three competitors, the Roeddes' *Hymac, Tomboy II* and *Elusive,* skippered by Stan Davies, H.B. Barkes and Bill Morrow. Over the next few decades, a large contingent of RVYC members sallied forth to sail the rough waters of the Swiftsure as the race grew in popularity.

The rough conditions of the Swiftsure pitted boats against the sea as much as each other. In the mid-1950s, Ralph Farris's 47-foot sloop *Hawk* was on the final downwind leg, returning to Victoria under spinnaker. John Long, a member of the crew, recalls how an eye pad that held the spinnaker sheet block tore free of the deck. "It acted like a slingshot, and the block hit Ralph a glancing blow to the head." Bleeding, Farris went below to be tended to by crew member Dr. Seiriol Williams. After giving Farris a "stiff drink of whisky," Dr. Williams "with a sail-maker's needle and thread put a half dozen stitches into Ralph's scalp to close the wound. We sailed on to finish the race without further mishaps."

The club's famous racing brothers, Sid and Phil Miller (the inseparable two were known to many members as "Phid and Sil") with their home-built champion *Clear Sky.*

The Lapworth 36 *Winsome III*, owned by Ches and Winn Rickard, was a Swiftsure champion in 1961, 1962 and 1963.

James McVie photo, RVYC

The 1961 Swiftsure was won by the RVYC's *Winsome III,* skippered by Bonar Davis, a victory that "showed the yachting world that Vancouver sailors had depth as well as excellence." Built for veteran club member Ches Rickard, one of the club's top Star and Six Metre racers, *Winsome III* was a light-displacement, dinghy-hulled Lapworth 36. Rickard, an Air Canada pilot, assembled a crack crew: Gordie Inglis from Victoria, Vic Palmer from Maple Bay, Bob Lance and Rob Maddison from the mainland, as well as Ray Delaplace and Bonar Davis. Davis had started off sailing the Swiftsure in 1959, crewing for Pat Leslie on his new L36, *Tricia,* and in 1960, joined *Winsome III*'s crew in her first Swiftsure.

The partnership of Bonar Davis and Ches Rickard, with a winning crew and a winning design, made *Winsome III* a champion. "Reasoning that Swiftsure was rather like running the mile," they ran hard and stayed on course even at night. Davis explains that "Many boats, when it gets dark, don't have the feel for keeping them going in the right direction." But Rickard, as an airline pilot, "was also a crack navigator," so he navigated while Davis sailed "until they at least knew where

the mark was. Then Davis would turn in for some rest while Rickard took the helm." *Winsome III*'s 1961 victory came without Rickard aboard, however, as he was in the east for a training course. But he was on hand and at the helm in 1962, when *Winsome III* again took the Swiftsure trophy. It was the first time the same boat had won twice in succession. *Winsome III* won again in 1963, after a protest removed the first-place winner, the Seattle yacht *Thetis,* from the race.

In the 1962 Swiftsure, as the club's Philip Graham, in his yacht *Troubadour,* raced to the finish line, a knock-down nearly ended the race for him. As Graham describes it, "We came boiling through Race Passage on a dead run with spinnaker at the bursting point . . . once through the passage, sheets were trimmed and the yacht was brought around on a reach, heading straight for the finish at Victoria . . . then the squall hit and over she went . . . lifelines and all underwater. It was fun while it lasted . . . lines and nerves stretching to the breaking point . . . a mad scramble to slacken off . . . and she eased back into more or less of an even keel . . . Whew! No harm was done (except to nerves)." Meanwhile, down in the galley, veteran chef and

Mary Bower (*left*) and the
Seattle Yacht Club's *Diamond
Head*—literally head to head—
approach the finish line at the
1966 Swiftsure. In a dramatic
conclusion, *Mary Bower*
surged ahead and won by a
6-foot lead.

sailor J.R. "Buzz" Buzzelle was cooking his traditional suckling pig dinner for the crew. Already a
club legend for his wild antics and fabulous meals,
for serving the crews Grasshoppers in silver gob-
lets before the race and for his love of firearms
(serving for years as the club's master gunner),
Buzzelle was not ruffled by *Troubadour*'s near cap-
size. As the yacht pulled into Victoria harbour, he
emerged from below with the suckling pig perched
perfectly on a silver platter, apple in its mouth.

The RVYC's pride, always maintained by its boats
and crews who participated in each year's Swiftsure,
swelled again in 1966 when the club's Swiftsure
veteran *Mary Bower,* skippered by John Long,
raced *Diamond Head* "in a gruelling thirty-five
hour endurance contest, where gale force winds
whipped up steep 12-foot seas, retiring almost half
the eighty-seven entries with blown-out sails, rig-
ging failure, sprung planks and dismastings."
Brought to Vancouver in 1956 by the RVYC's Ken
McRae, who restored the 1939-built English yacht,
Mary Bower remained with him until 1962, when
he sold her to John Long, who modified her in
1964 and assembled a crack crew. That crew—
Long, Alex Harrison, Doug Race, Steve Tupper,

Mary Bower's tired but triumphant crew, winners of the 1966 Swiftsure. *Top, left to right:* Steve Gill, Doug Race and Alex Harrison. *Bottom, left to right:* Ron Maitland, John Long (skipper), Dave Miller and Steve Tupper.

Facing page: Powering to the race start on English Bay in 1966. *Left to right: Troubadour, Hawk* and *Alciom.*

Dave Miller, Ron Maitland (a third-generation RVYC sailor) and Steve Gill—campaigned hard, starting in 1965. The effort paid off in 1966, when the race's historians proclaimed that year's Swiftsure "really belongs to *Mary Bower,* her untiring skipper, and her inspired young crew." The thirty-five-hour race was one of perseverance and good sailing, never overpowering the boat but letting her cut through the foreshortened waves and, as Dave Miller notes, changing the headsails "twenty or more times on the way to the lightship."

Diamond Head was in the lead as they left Victoria, but the two boats traded the lead, with *Mary Bower* first past Race Rocks and first around the lightship. A rip in the spinnaker on the return nearly spelled disaster, but *Mary Bower*'s crew hoisted the No. 1 genoa, patched the spinnaker and rehoisted it with a prayer that it would hold. They lost the lead after Race Rocks, even though *Diamond Head* blew out her last spinnaker, but Long and his crew kept on, even as the winds light-

ened. As they closed, neck and neck, Long stayed farther from shore, where the wind was stronger and at a better angle, spinnaker billowing. They passed very close to the end of the breakwater and won by a few feet and one second. *Mary Bower* and crew continued to race, winning the overall Swiftsure in 1969, but to this day, it is that picture-perfect finish in 1966 that remains vivid in most people's memories.

THE POWER BOATERS

While sail racing grew, so too did the motor vessel fleet. The postwar years were a boom time for motorboats, and designers like Ed Monk and Thornton Grenfell turned out scores of boats for club members. Monk, a Seattle designer, knew the B.C. coast very well, and a number of RVYC boaters turned to him for plans. The boats were built in local yards, notably George McQueen's on the Fraser River. The partnership between Monk and McQueen was so strong that some brokers

THE SIX METRE CLASS

From 1952 to 1962, the dominant one-design class in the Pacific Northwest was the Six Metre Class. Sandy Martin brought the first Six to arrive at the RVYC in 1952. His enthusiasm "made him the driving force of the soon-to-be fleet," according to David Williams. Martin sold his first Six, *Alana,* to Ches Rickard in 1954 and bought his second Six, *Hecate.* The racing Miller brothers, Sid and Phil, imported the third Six, *Ca Va,* followed by *Kini* (a syndicate boat owned by Doug Maitland, Lawrence Culter, Peter Evans and Bill Dolmage), and then Bob Day and Denny Wotherspoon's *Juno.* The sixth Six, Lorne Kyle's *Golden Hind,* arrived in 1955.

The Vancouver Sixes were locked in fierce competition with the Seattle's fleet of fourteen. Three Sixes from Victoria and an occasional visitor from California livened up the races at the Pacific International Yachting Association regattas. One of the Seattle Sixes, *Yillium,* was famed for the "gorgeous blonde daughter of the owner," according to Dave Williams. "She did foredeck duty, usually in a bikini, which everyone said was an effort to distract the rest of the fleet. It certainly did!" There was

also the challenge of the races, which were not just limited to a closed course. "These open cockpit boats did some of the classic gulf races where the water is over your head and the lights go out at night." The rewards were many, including the "barrel party," where the loser of the regatta paid to fill a beer keg with one third vodka, one third grapefruit juice and one third ginger ale. "The Americans always had to bring the vodka since it was illegal in British Columbia at the time; something to do with it being odourless and therefore the favoured drink when the cops were out."

The decline of the Sixes began in 1962 as new classes entered the various yacht clubs. The last major event was in 1970, when a match race challenge on English Bay pitted a visiting Six from the St. Francis Yacht Club against the RVYC's *Yam Sing.* The visitor, *St. Francis IV,* ultimately carried the day, winning the first three of five planned races. The last remaining Six in the club, the Miller brothers' *Ca Va,* has been rebuilt and still sails English Bay.

coined the term "Monk-McQueen" for the yachts they turned out—with repeat customers following the trends they set, including a gradual increase in the size of the powerboats from 38-footers up to 70-footers. Another builder, A.C. Benson Shipyards of Coal Harbour, also turned out Ed Monk's boats, starting with *Brenhines II* in 1959 for Robert Osborne. So many of these powerboats ended up in the rolls of the RVYC that some members feel that the club kept most of the local designers and builders in business. Member Baird Tewksbury recalls that the club was "part and parcel of the boating industry ... we have owned over half of the

Grenfells, and the same thing for the McQueens."

The postwar years saw the number of boats on the Pacific coast grow to 168 per cent higher than prewar statistics. Part of the appeal was the discovery by many families that powerboats were ideal for family cruising because of far more comfortable amenities—like showers, larger galleys and bunks—than previously had been available or would be found on a sailing yacht. Comfort, the ability to bring the kids, the power to travel faster and not rely on the wind induced some sailors to trade in their boats for motor yachts. The boom in powerboats also brought new members into the

Four Ed Monk-designed sister boats on their sea trials in Vancouver Harbour, 1961. *Left to right: Lady Diane, Dorlen* (later *Escalante*), *Breezin Thru* (later *Sequoia Park*) and *Brenhines III* (later *Keo Keo*).

RVYC, while elsewhere, new clubs were springing up, marinas were expanding and a new postwar phenomenon—the "Boat Show"—was inaugurated to market boating to the masses. The power boaters ended up being the club's largest group of rovers, ranging up and down the coast to Alaska, and sometimes into the Caribbean.

In 1957, a short account of the RVYC noted: "There are many members interested primarily in power boating. The powerboat fleet is quite extensive and includes such fine vessels as the *Norsal* owned by the Gibson brothers, the *Senarieta II* owned by Past Commodore Tom Ayres, *Casa Mia*

owned by the Reifel brothers, *Lazee Gal* by Joe Wilkinson, *Mamita* by Dr. R.E. McKechnie, *Invader* by F.B. Brown, *Bali Hai* by George Morgan, *Marijean* by H.R. MacMillan and many others. While the total membership of the club is now 1,450 the active and voting membership is limited to 500."

Norsal, built in 1921–22 by Menchions at Coal Harbour for N.R. Lang, manager of the Powell River Company, was in its time "the largest power yacht of its type" at 132 feet in length and a 19-foot beam. Powered by twin 200-horsepower Fairbanks-Morse diesels, *Norsal* flew the RVYC burgee and

Norsal, the famous Gibson brothers' yacht, one-time flagship of the RVYC, was well known for the liberal hospitality dispensed aboard.

POWERBOAT DESIGN

Past Commodore Robert Gibson, an enthusiastic power boater (and owner of four Ed Monk–designed boats, all named *Gibson Gal*) explained to Bet Oliver, author of *Ed Monk and the Tradition of Classic Boats*, why he consistently turned to Ed Monk for his boats: One of Ed Monk's greatest assets was his knowledge of boating in the Pacific Northwest. Ed designed layouts for the sometimes very wet weather, and hence more inside space, and less outside deck spaces. I have always credited Ed with two inno-vative Northwest features on his boats, namely the swim [grid] or rear boarding platform, and the rear gate from the cockpit to the boarding platform. In the Northwest, once we leave major areas, all boating is done by anchoring in secluded areas, when the dinghy is brought to the stern, and we get out the gate, onto the platform, and into either the dinghy or swimming! Very simple, but a terrific idea.

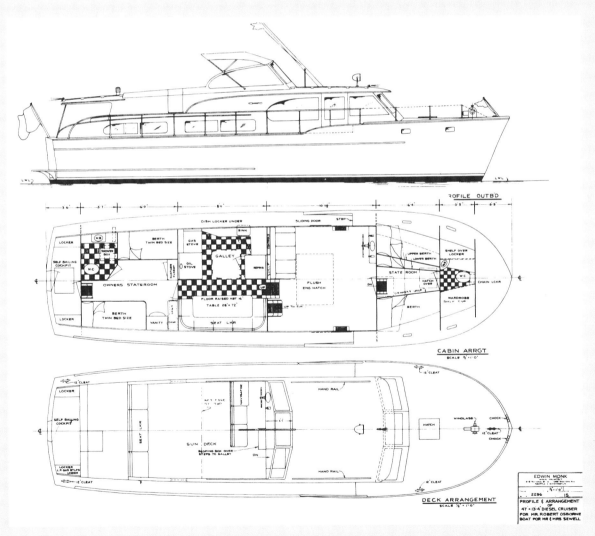

Drawings by Ed Monk for a 47-foot bridge-deck cruiser, *Brenhines III* built for the RVYC's Robert Osborne by Benson Shipyard of Vancouver in 1961.

From *Brochure of Pleasure Boat Design*, by Edwin Monk, courtesy of Edwin Monk Jr.

Tom Trapp's *Smitty* is a three-decade veteran of many predicted log racing competitions that exemplify the postwar activities of the club's power boaters, along with roving the coast on extended cruises.

made regular runs between Vancouver and Powell River until the Gibson brothers bought her in 1952. The Gibsons—Clarke, Jack, Earson and Gordon—were larger-than-life legendary businessmen and boaters. Gordon, the famous "Bull of the Woods," colourfully described the clan in his autobiography: "My three brothers and I have been in every kind of business except running liquor or owning a whorehouse. We have had opportunities for adventure as few other men of our generation, in gold mining, fishing, logging, construction, whaling and later politics." The Gibsons owned more than fifty vessels over the years, including the famous *Malahat,* a five-masted schooner that gained notoriety as the "mother ship" of rum row off the California coast during Prohibition, well before the Gibsons bought her and converted her into a log-carrying barge.

Clarke Gibson convinced his brothers to buy *Norsal* for their fishing fleet. As Gordon recalled, "He made a fine pitch, telling us how cheaply she would run as a fish packer and that she only used 10 gallons of diesel fuel an hour at twenty cents a gallon. But as soon as we saw her we knew she was far too fine to be run as other than a yacht, so we

kept her for pleasure—for fishing derbies with our friends." *Norsal* ended up with the Gibsons for twenty-five years. "It turned out that fuel has nothing to do with the running costs of a yacht," Gordon reminisced. "If our engines had run on Scotch whiskey and the guests had drunk diesel fuel we would have been better off." The Gibsons loaned out *Norsal*, under the command of her veteran skipper, William George Wyborn, for use as a training vessel for naval cadets from HMCS *Discovery* and for the RVYC's Junior Training Program, and when Clarke Gibson became commodore, as the club's flagship. Bill Botham, who took a cruise in *Norsal* to Silva Bay as a teenager in the 1950s, still remembers it as "fantastic." The yacht remained in the club through the 1970s, passing from Clarke to Earson and, finally, to Gordon Gibson Sr., who sold her in 1977.

BUILDING UP THE CLUB

The RVYC celebrated its fifty-year anniversary in 1953 on the brink of change. The Junior Training Program, the changing role of women in the club—an honorary life membership was awarded to a woman for the first time in 1955, to Ernestine

In 1966, the RVYC bestowed an honorary life membership to its oldest surviving founding member, Oswald "Skipper" Moseley. Commodore Doan Hartnell presented the award to Mr. and Mrs. Moseley.

Above: Temple "Sir Temp" Wright served as commodore in 1961 and 1962.

Below: Sir Temp's plaque noting the reserved spot at his table remains in place as a reminder of his powerful personality and contributions to the club.

"SIR TEMP"

One of the more colourful commodores of the postwar period was Temple Hall Wright, otherwise known as "Sir Temp." The long table in the clubhouse's Model Room bears an engraved plaque that marks his favourite seat at the head of a long table, proclaiming "Sir Temp" for all to see. Any member found sitting there by Temp Wright would be asked to vacate, "in no uncertain terms," according to Jock Ferrie, as this was his seat where he held court.

The more informal, family and fun-oriented postwar period and the club's traditions were lovingly lampooned for the 4 May 1963 Sail Past.

In 1976, the club hosted a Senior Members' Commemoration Dinner. Attendees included (*left to right*) Art Jefferd (joined 1909), Clarence Wallace (1914), Tom Ramsay (1907), Claude Thicke (1906), Gordon Farrell (1908) and Colin Ferrie (1916).

"Ernie" Jefferd, wife of long-time member Art Jefferd—and the increased activity on the water, all were indications of a new era. The 1960s and '70s were years of great change for both Vancouver and the Royal Vancouver Yacht Club. According to historian Robert A.J. MacDonald, these were the years when Vancouver "began to shed its image as a 'village at the edge of the rain forest' and to develop the attributes of a big city." The club, described in 1955 as "one of our town's most tradition-steeped sportive organizations," faced up to the challenges of the era and became more than a local yachting organization. By 2001, as the club approached its centennial, it would be described as the "sailing capital of western Canada," with an "international reputation for excellent race management and sailing instruction."

The years of growth were not without pain and controversy. The RVYC's annals describe tough decisions, measures for "increased efficiency" in its operations, special meetings and debates, and bold moves to build up its equity, at times in the face of opposition from within and outside the club. The first changes came in the late 1950s and continued through the '60s as the club made addi-

tions and modernized the Jericho clubhouse, after debating and setting aside plans for a new building in 1961. One debate that rocked the club was the battle over floating outdoor shelters for boats at Coal Harbour.

Coal Harbour, site of the RVYC's original quarters, had by 1957 become the primary moorage for most of the motorboats, or the "mahogany gin palaces," as Bob Gibson terms them. To protect the boats against the weather, a few boatsheds had been built, but the "somewhat unsightly collection of miscellaneous structures" was, in the minds of several of the power boaters, not enough. In 1957, as Commodore Elmer Palmer took the helm, Bob Gibson and twelve other power boaters convened downtown and, under the terms of the constitution, called a special meeting to demand that the club approve a regular program to build new shelters. The club's executive agreed to the terms of "we thirteen," Gibson recalls, which saw each of the power boaters contributing to pay for the new shelters as an advance "lease" for twenty years, after which the club would own the shelters outright.

The shelters made a great addition to the Coal Harbour facility, but it took some time for passions

Left: A killer gust of 60-knot winds hit RVYC member George O'Brien's *Mir* just a few hundred feet from the finish line at the 1969 Transpac. This aerial view was taken just seconds before the wind dismasted *Mir*.

Above: Undaunted by *Mir*'s dismasting, George O'Brien quickly jury-rigged his mizzen spinnaker to billow out and drag *Mir* across the finish line—stern first.

Pacific Yachting Collection

GEORGE O'BRIEN

Among the RVYC's most colourful members is George O'Brien, Jr., famed for his backward sail across the finish line at the Transpac, a series of other adventures and his "1000 horsepower personality." Club historian Jock Ferrie recalls one O'Brien adventure he personally witnessed in October 1959:

"It was an unusually warm sunny Vancouver day, and I was a guest of a friend for lunch at the Vancouver Lawn Tennis Club when I spied my old friend, the ever-engaging George O'Brien, at the bar. He told me that I would not believe who his guests were. 'Try me,' I said. 'Well, it's Errol Flynn and party.' 'Go on,' I said, 'not my hero, the swashbuckling Captain Blood of film fame.' 'The one and only,' said George. 'What the hell are you doing with him?' George told me Flynn had a beautiful large yacht called *Zaca* for sale, and he was in serious negotiations to purchase it. This stood to reason, as one thing George did well was buy fine yachts.

"As we were talking, the club secretary approached George and *sotto voce* said, 'Mr. O'Brien, your guests Mr. Flynn and party are at the front door. 'Well,' said George, 'send them right up.' 'No, Mr. O'Brien, we have a problem with that as Mr. Flynn is in his bare feet and furthermore he is in shorts and has no shirt.'

"'Well, I'll fix that,' said George. 'I'll take him to the pro shop and kit him out.' The club secretary said, 'We have another issue with Mr. Flynn. He has in each hand a 26-ounce bottle of Wolfschmidt vodka, which he absolutely refuses to part with.' George left to deal with his guests.

"About twenty minutes later, our hero, the now not-so-dashing Mr. Flynn, arrived in the dining room, suitably dressed, I was sure, at considerable expense by George. Trailing Flynn was his latest item, the beautiful teenage starlet Beverly Aadland and her mother, Florence. I never did find out how far the negotiations progressed, but the deal was never concluded as Flynn died a few days later while still in town."

The postwar period saw the introduction of a number of foreign bottoms, some of them famous, like the Norwegian "gold ship" *Gometra*, shown here driving to win. She was owned by four club members at various times: Elmer Palmer, Ken Glass, Gus Ortengren and Robert Butt.

James McVie photo, RVYC

to die down. As Lyall Bell recalls, it was a good thing, but "most of us had a hell of a time getting it together" to pay for them, and, as Gibson notes, some of the members "didn't speak to we thirteen for some time." The battle of the boatsheds was followed by a modernization of Coal Harbour in 1966-67: dredging, adding new floats and reorganizing the moorage, in part because the Vancouver Parks Board, ever eager to dispossess the club from its parklands, discovered that Stanley Park and the club had overlapping leases that left the area between high and low tide in each other's hands. Rather than engage in a battle with the Parks Board, the club decided to remove its foreshore structures and place everything on floats.

But that didn't mean that the RVYC always rolled over when the Parks Board tried to diminish the club's long-standing presence in Stanley Park. Past Commodore F.R. "Bill" Killam wrested one concession—continued parking at Coal Harbour—from the Parks Board through the clever acquisition of a key water lot. As Dave Williams recalls, "The club originally had the water lot lease in front of our neighbouring tennis club but lost it to the tennis club when it came up for renewal. So Bill arranged to acquire the water lot lease for the foreshore of what is now Jericho Beach! The Parks Board was appalled, but at a meeting aboard *Porpoise III* (the powerboat version), a compromise was reached whereby RVYC gave up the foreshore in front of Jericho Beach in exchange for parking in Coal Harbour."

Meanwhile, in spite of improvements to the clubhouse, many members had serious problems with the Jericho location. The moorage in front of the clubhouse left boats exposed in the winter. While in the past most boats had been shifted in the winter to Coal Harbour's more protected moorage, the growth of the club left boats, as well as its floats, vulnerable. Plans to protect the English Bay anchorage dated back to the mid-1920s, with a promise from the federal government to build a breakwater because the Harbour Commission planned to ban pleasure boats from the working harbour. But the Depression and war intervened. Plans for a breakwater were advanced in 1964

Hawk, the fastest of the famous Bird boats, was owned by J.C. McPherson. Here, she's tied up to a log boom at Centre Bay during a weekend cruise in 1961. The boat is still in the RVYC fleet and is owned by Ron Vines.

In 1960, an RVYC crew—Colin Park, Ken Baxter, Dave Miller and Bob Lance—took home the Sears Cup after competing at Green Lake, Wisconsin. The identity of the man in the middle is not known.

Facing page: With Sid Miller crewing, son Dave Miller skippers their champion Flattie, *Silver Wings*

The Wild Ride of the Sixes

One of the great tales of the sea and of sea rescue in the history of the club dates back to 7 May 1955, when a storm on the Strait of Georgia caught ten boats racing around Entrance Island. As Fleet Captain Peter Evans describes it:

"There were ten starters: the Eight Metre *Fulmar*, the five Six Metres *Alana, Golden Hind, Hecate, Juno* and *Kini;* the Roeddes' *Elusive* and Len Murrell's *Treveda;* and *Hereandthere* and *Barracouta II* in B Class. The distance from Jericho around the island and back is about 42 miles and, in the light going, the fleet was soon widely dispersed. By mid-afternoon the Eight and most of the Sixes were around the island, when a light breeze came in from the south and held. Shortly after seven o'clock, a bank of very dark cloud and a well-defined black line on the water were seen approaching from up the gulf, but most people paid little heed. Sudden and violent storms are relatively unknown in this area, particularly in the early summer, but a screaming inferno, in the space of a minute or two, covered the gulf from Point Grey to Nanaimo.

"When the storm first struck, the wind was about NNW, and it caught those with spinnakers set almost straight abeam. Picture nine small boats, several of them virtually open, many with spinnakers flying, and all with crews abruptly aroused from a very leisurely downwind run, trying to douse or reduce sail in a wind of at least 35 m.p.h. and increasing every moment, and a sea rapidly building up to unpleasant proportions, and you will have some idea of what it was like.

"On *Juno*, Denny Wotherspoon and Gordie Baker were on the foredeck, trying to get the spinnaker down, when a sheet or guy parted and the sail took charge. Before they knew what had happened, they were both in the water, with their ship sailing away from them. Bob Day, the skipper, and Herbie Millham, his only remaining crew member, threw the life ring overboard, but it went downwind so fast it was soon out of sight. At the same time, they were trying to bring the ship under control and sail her back to the rescue. By dint of fine seamanship and some superhuman work by Herbie, Bob succeeded in finding his two crewmen in the rapidly gathering dusk and got them aboard.

"The wind gradually backed through nor'west to WNW, becoming almost due west as the boats got farther in towards English Bay. It blew harder until the strength was such that speeds in excess of 58 m.p.h. were recorded in the gusts at the airport ...

"The problem of what to do after the race was over came in for some comment during the dash to the finish, and one skipper is reported to have yelled across to the other, enquiring how the h__ they were supposed to stop these bl__ things after the race was over. But stop they did, of course. [Bob Day ran *Juno* up 'on a fairly smooth-looking spit' on the North Shore under the First Narrows Bridge.]

"And like yacht racers everywhere, this exciting tale became food for many of their later discussions in this clubhouse, where, in the shelter of pleasant surroundings, all could tip their cups and treat their palates while sharing a constant passion for the sea."

during the tenure of Commodore Killam, but "politics," as Bob Gibson terms it, got in the way, including opposition from neighbours and the city's intervention against the breakwater. "We were losing members left and right," recalls Gibson. The West Vancouver Yacht Club, established in December 1945 in sheltered Fisherman's Cove on the North Shore, was attracting away RVYC members. The club "would have failed without that breakwater," and a 1968 storm that damaged the docks during Commodore T.F. "Bill" Orr's tenure finally pushed the matter to a head.

In spite of protests from the City of Vancouver, which originally had approved the breakwater but then changed its mind and tried to stop the plans, the club was able to proceed, thanks to the fact that it leased the 12.49-acre water lot in front of the clubhouse from the province, so the city had no jurisdiction. Designed by club member J.S.

"Jack" Wood, a marine engineer, the new breakwater was built of piles, instead of wider, bulkier rock, to maximize the tight quarters of the lot. After the official opening in November 1970, work on the breakwater and new floats continued, with an increase from 190 berths in 1971 to 322 berths in 1985. The results were gratifying. Thanks to the new facilities and a push that acquired offshore stations, the club's membership flourished in the next few decades.

Beyond These Shores

"We are a multifaceted club. Our membership ranges from world-class sailors to family cruising members. Our interests vary from one-design racing to offshore cruising. Our pride in the Royal Vancouver Yacht Club unites us all." –Commodore A. J. Patrick Oswald, 1985

The RVYC's offshore stations were the direct result of Bob Gibson's taking careful note of a film, screened at the club in the spring of 1960, that showed a New York Yacht Club offshore station in Long Island Sound. Upon learning that these had become a powerful incentive for boaters to join that club, Gibson went before the RVYC's executive, all fired up about the concept. The executive agreed, granting him permission to find property in the Gulf Islands for no more than $5,000. After touring the area aboard Bob Day's motor yacht *Malecite,* a group of members that included Ron Runge, Penn Taylor and Lyall Bell finally decided on Tugboat Island. They convinced

Facing page: Fred Long's *Fox Hound*, winner of Boat of the Year at the RVYC for 1987, 1988, 1989, 1990 and 1991.

Commissioning Day in 1986 at the club's offshore station at the Wigwam Inn. The post-war program that created the stations was a significant undertaking that greatly enhanced the club's assets while promoting unparalleled growth in the membership.

Milt Goodman photo

the membership at a special meeting to buy it for $27,000, with each member assessed $36 to pay for it. It was a difficult proposition to sell, as a number of members were wary of the purchase. It was too far away, said some, while others worried about the long-term liability. As it was, recalls Jack Christensen, the approval vote just "squeaked past."

The next offshore station, purchased in 1965, was Alexandra Island, off Gambier Island in Howe Sound, a property owned by Past Commodore Barney Johnson and leased to the club. In keeping with the new push for club-owned offshore stations, Commodore Lyall Bell began to negotiate with Johnson. Years later, Bell recalls how he brought the sale to a close. Johnson was asking for $30,000, but the club could not afford that. Finally, Bell decided to make an appointment to see Johnson at the old commodore's West End home. After work, Bell drove home to change into his yacht club uniform, then went to Coal Harbour to retrieve his hat from his boat. Only then, properly kitted out, did he knock on Johnson's door. The butler answered and led Bell in. Mrs. Johnson was there, wearing a yacht club uniform, and, as Barney Johnson entered, Bell noted that he, too,

was in uniform—full sea-going kit, right there in his living room. Johnson took one look at Bell, turned to his wife and said, "See, I told you the commodore would know enough to dress properly." They sat down, and the butler brought Bell and Barney a Westward Ho. "You get only one, Mr. Commodore," Barney told his guest, and then settled down. The price for the island was $15,000 and "no more." When Bell asked about the additional $15,000, Johnson replied, "I wanted to see what kind of deal I could get from you." Bell's last-minute decision to wear his uniform had won Alexandra Island for the club by appealing to the grand old man's sense of tradition.

The program of buying offshore stations continued through the next three decades. The stations were improved thanks to dedicated work and donations from members, starting with the first work party at Tugboat Island in November 1960, when a crew of volunteers redecked the dock and raised a flagstaff. Jack Christensen, well known for his love of the sea, sailing and philanthropy, managed the major lumber mill at Tahsis, and he donated bundles of cedar logs to form a floating breakwater. Work on Tugboat continued through

Facing page: The club's Wigwam
Inn offshore station.

Fifer, still going strong more
than six decades after her launch.

In the best traditions of the club's power boaters and their extending rovings up the coast, Ron Cliff's *Sea Q* (*left*) and Bob Brodie's *Horizon V* rendezvous in Alaska.

Facing page: The RVYC's Cortes Bay offshore station by moonlight.

the decade, with more tasks for volunteers added after the acquisition of Alexandra Island.

In 1970, the club added a third offshore station when it purchased property in Secret Cove on the Sunshine Coast from Bob and Bill Orr, Bob Gibson, Loring Foster, P.R. "Gunner" Wilson and Alex Healey. This new station provided the first sheltered area for boats heading north along the Sunshine Coast and became a popular moorage on the way to Desolation Sound. The first work done was driving pilings, and that winter Bob Orr used his boat *Owaissa* to tow the station's new 350-foot float from Coal Harbour, arriving to find half an inch of ice covering the bay. Nevertheless, Orr manoeuvred the float into place, using his boat as an icebreaker. A souvenir of his donation to the cause was deep scoring on the boat's unprotected bow. That level of dedication was a reflection not only of the value that members set on the offshore stations but their love of these places. Another typical story of work at Secret Cove, apart from

the annual cleanup and painting work parties, was the two-day redecking of the float in 1985 by an eight-man crew led by Jack Charles. Another eleven members assisted, hauling new lumber, clearing and burning old lumber, placing non-skid wire on the boardwalk and installing the water system.

The fourth offshore station, Scott Point on Saltspring Island, provided another Gulf Island stopping-off point when the club bought it in April 1977. "A true resort," with a pavilion, a swimming pool, cottages that members could rent, an anchorage (protected by a stone rip rap breakwater donated by Jack Charles) and dock facilities, again built and maintained thanks to the work parties of dedicated members, made the new station a very popular addition.

The next offshore station was the historic Wigwam Inn, on northern Burrard Inlet at the headwaters of Indian Arm, built in 1906 as a "luxury resort lodge in the wilderness." It had changed

The 62-foot *Starfire*, a Bill
Garden design, was built in the
1960s at the Philbrook yard
in Sidney on Vancouver Island
and is now owned by member
Jamie Angus.

Facing page: The 42-foot
Mistigris, one of the famous
Italian Rivas brought to Canada
by the club's Frank Griffiths,
was one of ten powerboats
owned by him. *Mistigris* made
the fastest passage on record
from Juneau, Alaska, on a
cruise.

hands several times through the years. Once more, a committee that included Past Commodore Bob Gibson worked its magic, negotiating with the bank and acquiring the 17,000-square-foot building and surrounding 156 acres in April 1985 for $220,000—a fraction of its value. Under the guidance of Ralph Jordan (who later served as commodore in 1989), work parties hastily readied the new station, constructing docks and quarters for the caretakers, rebuilding the seawall, upgrading the electrical and water systems, and cleaning up the grounds. These and many other tasks took thousands of hours and yet were completed in time for the official commissioning of Wigwam as the fifth offshore station on 23 June 1985—little more than two months after its acquisition.

The club added two more properties—Garden Bay in Pender Harbour and Cortes Bay on Cortes Island, at the entrance to Desolation Sound (the latter shepherded by Past Commodore R.S. "Bob" Butterfield since its inception)—filling out the number of offshore stations to seven. These outstanding facilities, in the words of Bob Gibson, are "well worth the price of membership." In fact, they constitute the single greatest factor in the club's later success. Many agreed with Gibson about the value of the stations to members, because between 1971 and 1985, membership grew by a phenomenal 60 per cent.

The offshore stations have become such a crucial part of the RVYC's life that many members would find it hard to imagine a club without them.

John Newton's *Princess Pachena*,
a 70-foot Canoe Cove, was the
last boat built at the Sidney,
B.C., yard. The boat has spent
many summers roving Alaskan
waters and remains in the RVYC
fleet.

The stations have their own "mayor," or member in charge, and most have dedicated staff caretakers. Each year, members form work parties to improve and maintain them. The stations are a favourite destination for families, with cruises to them ending with barbecues and events that fill the days and evenings with camaraderie and fun that exemplify how much the roving lifestyle of the club, for both the sailors and the power boaters, has been enhanced by them. The deep personal commitment of a number of individuals throughout the years not only has built up an impressive group of properties and facilities but also has placed the offshore stations at the centre of club life.

BLUE WATER CRUISING AND RACING

In the late 1950s, the club's sailors began to extend their activities well beyond local shores. The booming economy meant that members could afford bigger boats, and the idea of ocean racing and "blue water cruising" out into the Pacific—and beyond—attracted their attention. They began to participate in races like the Transpac—an open ocean run from Long Beach to Honolulu. In 1959, Phil Graham "started to toy with the idea of going in

the Honolulu Race. However, the one thing that really was holding me back was the lack of experience on the open ocean." In 1960, Graham and Otis Lamson of Seattle organized a new race they called the Norpac, from the mouth of the Columbia River up the Washington coast to Port Angeles. Although the "weather was quite severe," the "experience gained in that race laid the groundwork for our Honolulu trip." Graham entered his yacht *Troubadour* in the 1961 Transpac, and in 1962 tackled both the Swiftsure and Norpac races.

The Transpac caught the eye of other RVYC sailors, and Graham soon found himself competing not only with American yachts but also those of fellow club members. In 1969, one club sailor made Transpac history by sailing across the finish line backwards. George O'Brien, a member since 1948, sailed his 87-foot ketch *Mir* hard across the Pacific, blowing out four sails during the race. As *Mir* approached the end of the line, in Molokai Channel, in third place, a sudden gust heeled her over, and the mainmast came crashing down. Not to be defeated, O'Brien and his crew cleared away the debris, set a spinnaker on the mizzenmast and

The 63-foot Thornton Grenfell–built *Lazee Gal*, commissioned by the Wilkinson family, and later owned by Ben Dueck and Clark Bentall, is now owned by David Bentall.

Lol Killam's famous *Graybeard* was no beauty, but with him at the helm, she cruised the world on many adventures, carrying the flag of the RVYC to distant ports.

James McVie photo, courtesy of the Killam family

sailed backwards across the finish line to retain their third-place standing. O'Brien went on to head the Canadian Challenge Syndicate for the America's Cup and purchased Australia's 1967 America's Cup challenger, *Dame Pattie,* bringing her to Vancouver. There, renamed *Endless Summer,* she won the 1970 Swiftsure and was the basis for the Royal Vancouver Yacht Club's being the challenger of record for the America's Cup in 1974. Difficulties with funding ended that challenge, but the club ended up participating in the famous cup races that year when Past Commodore Alex Forsyth was selected as the first Canadian judge for the America's Cup Eliminations.

Eager to establish a Hawaii race out of British Columbia, J.G. "Jim" Innes, a CP Air pilot who joined the club in 1959, with Lol Killam and others inaugurated a passage from Victoria to Lahaina, following the route of the old sailing ships that once regularly connected British Columbia and Hawaii. In 1965, P.R. "Dick" Sandwell chaired the inaugural "race," actually more of a cruise, between three yachts, won by Innes in his *Long Gone.* The idea caught on. In 1968, the Royal Vancouver and the Lahaina Yacht Club formally established the race, held every other year and now known as the Vic-Maui. Vic-Maui fever swept through both clubs and, more than any other race, introduced RVYC members to the open ocean. Lol Killam fondly recalls his first Vic-Maui, which was in 1965 as one of the founders of that race, aboard his yacht *Velaris.* In a résumé of his favourite sailing experiences, he described it as "the most exciting, because it was my first ocean voyage under sail." In 1968, the news headline was "the battle of the Killam brothers in the Pacific." Bill Killam, in his new *Porpoise,* came in first in the Vic-Maui, and Lol came in second in *Velaris.*

Lol Killam went on to win the 1970 Vic-Maui in his new 73-foot yacht *Graybeard,* built in Richmond by Bill Killam's company, ICL Engineers. *Graybeard* completed the 2,308-mile passage in 15 days, 47

The Copeland Family: Sailing the World

Andy Copeland grew up on the Solent in the U.K. and started sailing in 1946 at age twelve. Later, during his time as a fighter pilot in the Royal Navy, he raced in national and international events and was in line to take over as skipper of the royal Dragon, *Bluebottle,* when it was decided to retire her. In 1966 he moved to the Caribbean, where he worked as a professional yacht captain and was a founder member of the Antigua Yacht Club. He was twice Caribbean Sailfish Champion and represented Antigua in three Sunfish World Championships.

Andy met Liza in Venezuela in 1971, when both were racing. She had also grown up in England, sailing both in dinghies and ocean racers. They were married aboard the famous ketch *Ticonderoga,* and their honeymoon consisted of a week of racing in the Sunfish Worlds, then sailing across the Atlantic to Europe in *Eileen,* a 65-foot Fife yawl.

Settling in Vancouver in 1973, they purchased the first *Bagheera,* a 24-foot San Juan quarter-tonner, and joined the Royal Vancouver Yacht Club. Since then there have been several *Bagheera*s, whose successes include winning the VARC IOR Boat of the Year award, and the quarter ton and the three quarter ton IOR championships at PITCH.

Andy was asked in 1984 to deliver an Ocean 72-foot ketch from Vancouver to Hong Kong. A broken boom two thirds of the way across the North Pacific made a diversion necessary to tiny Wake Island. At this American military base, the yacht was arrested, cited as "the suspect vehicle used for the importation of Moroccan hashish into North Carolina in 1978." Different owners and a long time before, but the yacht was taken over and the crew repatriated by the U.S. Air Force.

In 1985 the current 40-foot *Bagheera* was built in France, and Andy and Liza, together with their young sons Duncan, Colin and Jamie, embarked on a cruise that turned into a circumnavigation lasting six years, logging over 50,000 nautical miles and visiting eighty-two countries and colonies. There were some exciting moments, including losing a rudder in Madeira, being chased in the Malacca Strait, being boarded by thieves at night in Zanzibar and being damaged by lightning off Mozambique. Liza wrote two successful books recounting these adventures.

In 1992, Andy and Liza each had their own Dragons at the club, participating in two Dragon World Championships and other events abroad. They cruised *Bagheera* in the Pacific Northwest until 1998, often skippered by Duncan, while Jamie was active in the club's junior racing program. Then Andy and Liza sailed to Nova Scotia, exploring both sides of North and Central America, and resulting in another book by Liza. In 2001 they crossed the Atlantic for the fourth time together and have since cruised in the Mediterranean. *Bagheera* is now eighteen years old and has logged just over 81,000 nautical miles.

The Vic-Maui, brainchild of club member Jim Innes, is a premiere racing event in the calendar of world yachting.

minutes and 45 seconds to win first to finish and first overall on corrected time. It was an auspicious start to a career that saw Lol and *Graybeard* sail the seven seas—and then some. Lol circumnavigated the globe in 1970-71 on an eleven-month, 32,000-mile voyage that began with the Vic-Maui win and continued on to include the Cape Town to Rio, where he came in second, and then the Transpac. Another extended voyage, in 1974-75, was an eleven-month, 15,000-nautical mile tour of the Pacific Rim, including the Sydney-Hobart Race. By 1980, Lol Killam had sailed more than 100,000 miles in *Graybeard,* and, as the *Vancouver Sun* reported, on those voyages had "basked in the tropics, swilled beer and settled bets with Aussies at Port Moresby in New Guinea, toasted to safe sea journeys with vodka in the company of Russian sailors at Nakhodka, made his peace with the Mozambique Channel in 60-knot winds." Summing up what he had learned in his

open water sailing, he said: "Sailors have a broader view of life than others. They face nature in the raw. It adds to a person's humility to go out and have a battle with the sea. You yourself become small if you thought you were big."

Peter Chettleburgh, who eulogized Lol Killam in 1988, after he died at age seventy-four, praised him as the "best skipper with whom I've ever sailed, consistent, patient and ever mindful of the boat and its crew... When you came aboard he would tell new crew members there were three ways to do things on *Graybeard*—your way, the right way and his way. He never left any doubt which was the right way." His family and fellow club members committed his ashes to the deep, and now part of Lol Killam remains forever part of the sea.

Another Vic-Maui veteran, John Long, winner of many races and commodore in 1976, competed in his first of five Vic-Maui races in 1968, never winning but revelling in the experience. As he

Lol Killam at the helm of his beloved *Graybeard*. Designed by local naval architect Peter Hatfield, *Graybeard* measures 68 feet on the waterline, 73 feet overall, draws 12 feet and displaces 83,000 pounds (of which 30,000 is the lead at the bottom of her fin keel). Rigged as a ketch with a 104-foot aluminum mast, she carries up to 8,000 square feet of sail.
Courtesy of the Killam family

explains: "Round the buoy racing is exhilarating, exciting and demanding. But I find the long trips are more satisfying to me—the beauty of the stars on a clear night on the high seas and watching the sun come up in the middle of the ocean. I feel sorry for those who have not had the opportunity to experience it."

Another veteran racer, John Newton, agrees, and his memories are "of the races I lost." Starting sailing in the early 1960s and crewing with Past Commodore Elmer Palmer and Pat Leslie, Newton sailed Davidson dinghies and recalls he was "always dead last against Bonar Davis, Gerry Palmer and the rest of the guys." He recalls how he won his first race, around Tugboat Island: he was lying in second place when he noticed the first-place boat sculling, so he protested and won the hearing. With more than a hundred races to his credit, and thirty-one Swiftsures, Newton travelled well beyond local shores, racing four times in the Admiral's Cup races in the U.K., starting in 1975 when he crewed on Vlad Plavsic's boat, and then three times on his own yacht *Pachena,* representing Canada.

In 1979, John Newton—with crew John Simonette, Doug Race, Steve Tupper, Stewart Jones, Glenn Shugg, Don Martin, Pat Leslie and Mike Schnetzler—competed in the Admiral's Cup in his *Pachena,* and during the Fastnet race was caught in a killer storm in mid-August. A 60-knot wind whipped up a Force 10 storm that battered the 303 boats racing toward Ireland 70 miles off the English coast. Forty-foot-high waves and howling winds capsized and dismasted ships, sank five yachts and led the owners of nineteen others to abandon them, with the loss of fifteen lives. Two miles off Fastnet, heavy seas hit *Pachena*. Newton recalls how the waves "would hit us, and the boat

Pachena, skippered by John Newton, survived the killer Force 10 storm at the 1979 Fastnet Race. Here, in the midst of the action, Doug Race takes the helm. Stewart Jones sits next to him, while Mike Schnetzler stands at the rail.
Courtesy of John Newton

would fall from the top of the wave—about 30 feet into the trough." Putting into Cork, Ireland, *Pachena*'s crew avoided the disaster that struck many others. Although "very disappointed we didn't complete the race," Newton says, "you have to balance the safety of the crew and the boat … I'm just glad were all alive and well." Undaunted, he went on to again represent Canada in the Admiral's Cup.

Blue water racing and cruising also got into the blood of Dick Sandwell, who started by racing the Transpac in his 48-foot sloop *Gabrielle II* in 1965. Sandwell, who in 1948 founded a small engineering company that "grew into one of the largest pulp and paper equipment manufacturers and contractors in the world," was a life-long yachtsman, and a lover of tales of ocean voyages and exploration. Throughout his life, he collected rare books and charts, building a wonderful library of early exploration and navigation. But as a boy in a dinghy with a homemade sail, his dream was to surge across the finish line in an ocean race.

In addition to his membership in the RVYC, Dick Sandwell was also, at the time of his death, the only Canadian member of the Royal Yacht Squadron at Cowes, as well as a member of the Royal Swedish Yacht Club. While he owned many yachts in his lifetime, his favourite—and ultimate—was *Gabrielle III*. Laid down with his requirements for "a comfortable cruiser for B.C. waters, but able to race without disgrace now and again," she was built on the banks of the Clyde to replace *Gabrielle II*, a wooden yawl he had bought in Sweden in 1959. Halfway through the Transpac, Sandwell decided that racing was not as much fun as cruising: "You wonder why on earth you put up with the noise, stench and fatigue for days on end … It was under these circumstances I decided to build a new boat for cruising, and to hell with racing!"

In spite of Sandwell's decision, the first four years of *Gabrielle III*'s life were spent racing, starting with the 1968 Vic-Maui. From there, he carried on to Polynesia and down to Australia to participate in the Sydney-Hobart race of 1968. Then, he shipped the yacht on a freighter to England, sailing in the Admiral's Cup races at Cowes in 1969. In 1970-71, he went on an extended cruise through Scandinavian, French and English waters, racing in the Gotland Runt and Skaw Races as well as enjoying European waters in a more leisurely fashion,

before finally shipping his yacht back to Vancouver. Once home, *Gabrielle III*'s "days of oceanwide wanderlust were over," but not Sandwell's. Henceforth, he and his family and friends spent the next two decades either cruising the vast inland waters of British Columbia and the west coast of Vancouver Island on *Gabrielle III,* utilizing Captain Vancouver's charts, or cruising more distant shores like the Mediterranean, Adriatic, Baltic and Caribbean in chartered yachts.

Dick Sandwell's sailing companions, crew and "camp followers," as he termed them in two beautiful, privately printed volumes of his voyages, included many other club members. One was local historian Jack Kendrick, who knew the voyages of the early navigators on the B.C. coast like the back

of his hand and who delighted with Sandwell in retracing them. Another, of course, was Agnete Sandwell, Dick's wife, who modestly protests to this day that she was "no yachtsman," though all who sailed with her fondly recall the magnificent job she did in provisioning the ship and looking after their guests—and ensuring that the skipper always had his pink gin fixings stocked up. Before he died in October 1996, Dick Sandwell had donated a number of trophies and prizes to the club, including the Sandwell Offshore Trophy in 1987, for the most notable offshore voyage, race or cruise completed each year. This elegant trophy, a framed original chart of Captain James Cook's discoveries in the Pacific, is an eloquent memorial to his love of the sea, its charts and literature.

Facing page: Racing on English
Bay in 1978.

P.R. "Dick" Sandwell at the helm
of *Gabrielle III*, offshore—one of
his favourite places to be.
Courtesy of Agnete Sandwell

The club's rovers have included the power boaters who now are the majority of the boat-owning membership. Robert G. "Bob" Brodie, who joined in 1960, exemplifies the members who embrace both sail and powerboats. Sailing in the first of sixteen Swiftsures in 1959, Brodie also crewed on the 1961 and 1967 Transpacs, raced as a Soling skipper (including the 1976 Olympic trials at Kingston), and in 1978 switched to Stars, winning several championships through the 1980s. During this period, he also owned a succession of inboard/outboard runabouts, including a 40-foot Tollycraft *Prelude*. In 1977 Brodie had a 72-foot Monk-McQueen, *Horizon V,* built, and she served as the club's flagship during his two years as commodore in 1978–79.

Brodie's successor, Commodore David R.L. Rolfe, was another sail and power boater. After joining as a junior in 1946, he raced Snipes, Lightnings and Stars, and acquired his first powerboat, a fourteen-foot inboard, *Daveth*. As an adult, he continued his passion for racing, crewing on three Swiftsures and many other races. Through the 1960s, Rolfe owned a series of three 17-foot runabouts before buying a 33-foot Enno-built powerboat, *Kanga*. In 1975, he acquired a 43-foot Monk-McQueen, *Banook*, which served as the club's flagship in 1980. Rolfe was succeeded as commodore by William T. "Bill" Kidner, a keen power boater who focussed his energies on predicted log races, with him and his *Totem Chief* serving as part of the winning Canadian team for

DeAnza III, a 65-foot Ted Drake design built in 1959 by Western Craft of North Vancouver, was a product of the classic postwar period of motorboat construction. Built for prominent local lumberman William S. Brooks, *DeAnza III* has also been owned in turn by Hubie Wallace, Phil Chutter and Gordon Levett.

Bob Brodie's *Horizon V*, a 72-foot Monk-McQueen, is now called *Ho-Aloha* and is owned by club members Jim and Linda Egerton.

The 70-foot yacht *Christabel*, one of Ed Monk Jr.'s early designs, was built by George McQueen for Ralph Smith around 1975. She is now owned by Reg Stranks.

Facing page: The 58-foot Monk-McQueen *Lanikai* was built for Lorne Yorke. She is now owned by John Morgan.

the Century 21 World's Fair Trophy in 1976 and 1977. As this brief look at these three commodores and their boats indicates, the club's membership has straddled the line between sail and power, and racing and roving, even as the postwar era witnessed the spectacular growth of interest in power boating.

The straddling of interests between sail and power has not always been easy, and the club's executive worked through the years to ensure balance. In 1982, the Women's Committee's president, Pauline Moan, appointed two members to specifically represent power boating on the committee's executive "to create a balance of ideas . . . allowing the Women's Committee to grow from what was becoming mainly a sailing group." Joyce MacCrostie-Shives, an active (and founding) committee member, recalls: "Because of opportunities and talents of lady skippers such as Rosemary Wright, Sue Liebert, Megan Balmer, Lynne Brown, Mary Light and many others, the women sailors dominated the membership. This was a natural happening, as active participation of women power boaters was much more limited in opportunities. We learned, we grew, and we enjoyed." The quest for balance also was evident in a variety of ways, including the creation of a stained-glass window for the clubhouse by Mrs. Eugene "Button" Killam in 1983, at the request of Commodore James C. "Jim" Heaney, to "represent RVYC's sail and power activities."

The 1980s and '90s saw the growth of power-boats—literally—as members who started with smaller boats gradually "traded up" to larger ones. Frank and Emily Griffiths owned, throughout their boating lives, more than ten powerboats, all of them "interesting one-offs," including the first Italian Rivas in Canada (one of them was one of the famous Aquarama speedboats), a converted World War II air-sea rescue craft, a fast 42-foot Sportfish, the 136-foot *Norango*—a boat in which the family enjoyed extended cruises from Vancouver to the Caribbean—and *LaFeline*, an 85-foot design with the speed and appearance of a French patrol gunboat while the interior "was every inch a high quality yacht."

Past Commodore Bill Botham and his wife, Kate, stayed with powerboats. As he recalls, "The Royal Vancouver Yacht Club has been a focal point for my family, with my father, Bill Botham Sr., having been a member of the club since 1948. Dad had a diverse collection of boats from a little 16-foot runabout to a 48-foot diesel, bridge deck motor yacht. He got me into the club as a junior in 1959. My wife Kate and I started boating in the early '70s in a 33-foot fibreglass production boat, but, as our family grew, so did the size of our boat. Our next boat was 34 feet, but this was quickly replaced by the first of our wooden boats, all being named *Deora* and all being Monk-McQueens. This first one was a 50-footer, followed three years later by a

Facing page: Lyall Bell's *Four Bells*, a 52-foot Monk-McQueen, has served as the RVYC flagship, ably representing it (and helping win the Wilson Trophy for Seamanship) at many Seattle Yacht Club opening days. She also hosted His Royal Highness Prince Andrew on a visit to the RVYC. The boat is now owned by Lyall's son Barry (himself a commodore in 1992).

Frank Griffiths's French-built *LaFeline* has gunboat-style lines that make her fast, but she is also a luxurious yacht that made many cruises to Alaska.

60-footer and then finally our current 75-footer. 'Two foot-itis' plus a bit! We became wooden boat fanatics quite early in our boating endeavours." Bill Botham calls the Monk-McQueens the "Bentley of the boat world," and he and his wife are on the water on *Deora* whenever possible, often cruising to Princess Louisa, whose preservation Bill remains deeply committed to as president of the Princess Louisa Inlet International Society.

Past Commodore Ronald Laird "Ron" Cliff also has a liking for Monk-McQueens. He started with a wooden 38-foot Tollycraft, then moved to Monk-McQueens with a 59-footer, his first *Sea Q*. Next came a 71-footer, then an 82-footer and,

finally, his current 88-foot fibreglass *Sea Q*.

The 1980s also witnessed the beginning of the era of the mega-yachts. The McQueens eventually got up to 85 feet when George McQueen started building on Westport fibreglass hulls. But the major jump came when RVYC member (and yacht builder) Jack Charles, owner of *Hotei*, an 80-foot Monk-McQueen, introduced the club to its first large contemporary yacht, a new *Hotei*. Launched in 1986, the 115-foot luxury yacht served as host vessel for Expo '86. *Hotei*, a famous host at sail pasts and other events, remains a club favourite and an inveterate cruiser, ranging from Juneau to Puget Sound.

Facing page: The 82-foot Monk-McQueen *Sea Q*, formerly owned by Ron Cliff, who was commodore in 1986. His current *Sea Q* is 88 feet long.

Club member Jack Charles's *Hotei*, a 115-foot Sarin design built by McQueen in 1986 inaugurated the era of the contemporary large boats.

Bill Botham, who was com-
modore in 2001, and his beloved
(and current) *Deora*, a 75-foot
Monk-McQueen, originally
built as *Mary J* for another past
commodore, Ralph Jordan.

Milt Goodman photo

Gibson Gal, a 75-foot Monk-McQueen built for Bob Gibson, is now owned by Gordon Cartwright.

Lorne Yorke's second *Lanikai* is
an 88-foot Monk-McQueen.

The 95-foot Defever-McQueen
Owaissa, built for R.A. "Bob" Orr.

A product of Thornton Grenfell's
yard, the 59-foot *Vandal*
was owned by Les Summers
and later by "Mac" Byrd.

A classic designed by Thornton
Grenfell, the 45-foot *Good
Ship*, owned by Milt Goodman,
at the 1980 RVYC Sail Past.
Jordan Welsh photo

Ralph Jordan and Milt Goodman working the barbeque at the Tugboat Island offshore station, around 1979.

Facing page: The RVYC's birthplace, Coal Harbour, today remains a major anchorage for the club's fleet of motor vessels.

A downwind spinnaker run at the World Dragon Championship in 1983.

A Period of Phenomenal Increase

Between 1970 and 1985, the Royal Vancouver Yacht Club underwent the most dramatic change in its history. The club returned to the Olympics after its initial 1932 foray with flair, starting with the 1956 Games and continuing through 1960, 1964, 1968 and 1972. Those years also witnessed a "phenomenal increase in membership, fleet, moorage facilities and the acquisition of offshore stations," as the club retired its $1.5 million debt and spent more than $5 million on its facilities. Membership grew to three thousand, with approximately a thousand boats.

The one-design classes saw significant achievements in the 1970s and beyond. The Dragons survived the loss of their Olympic status after twenty-five years of racing and thrived, with RVYC sailors competing in Dragon championships at every level. As Dragon racer and world champion Bob Burgess noted in 1986, "The thrill of sailing this classic yacht has brought together dozens of Royal Vancouver members, provided them with highest calibre one-design racing and lifetime friendships throughout the world."

The same held true for the Star Class, which had declined to only two or three boats at the club by 1971. But a gradual increase built up the Star fleet to a dozen boats by 1985, and they served as the platform for a series of club champions, like David Miller, Bill West, Mike Clements and Ross Macdonald. In 2003, the club's Star sailors marked eighty years of unbroken organized competitive sailing, which as they proudly note, "is an extraordinary accomplishment and one that cannot be transcended by any other global one-design class." By initiating consistent racing on English Bay, the Star sailors helped push the club into moving out of Coal Harbour's restricted waters, and thus, "When Jericho station was completed in 1927, Star members could look back with pride because they

A Racing Family: The Millers

Beginning in the 1930s, two members of the "talented sailing Miller family," brothers Phil and Sid Miller—joined by Sid's wife, Janet, and later by their son, David—made club and racing history. Sailing in 18-foot sloops known originally as Flatties and later as Geary 18's, Phil and Sid Miller captured the world championship in their Flattie *Silver Wings* in 1935. Phil Miller retained the championship in 1936 and 1937, and Sid Miller, sailing with wife Janet, held the title in 1938. David Miller, with father Sid crewing, won the championship in 1960, sailing the same *Silver Wings* with which Sid had won in 1935.

The Millers won races in Stars and Sixes as well. David Williams remembers how they showed up one day with their new Six, *Ca Va,* ready to race with a significant modification. "To avoid Six Metre sailing becoming a money game, the fleet adopted a policy of cotton sails only. The Millers shocked all the other Sixes in the fleet by appearing in a varnished main and jib that apparently worked very well without violating the rule of no synthetics."

Phil and Sid Miller's trophy collecting was summarized by club historian George A. Cran in 1981: "In 1940, they won the Roedde Star Fleet Championship in their Star *Clear Sky,* and on the resumption of racing after the war, they won this trophy again in 1946 and again in 1948. Their names are also on another Perpetual Club Cup—the Star Fleet Captains—which they won in 1947, '48, '50 and '51. They also won the famous Harry Wylie Shield with their *Clear Sky* in 1947 and in '48, and the Watt Trophy in '47, '48, '49. Graduating to a larger yacht

with *Ca Va,* they won the Stock Exchange Trophy in 1957, '58 and '60. Also in 1957, they won both the Gyles Trophy and the Juno Trophy."

Phil and Sid Miller built their own Flattie and Star boats, and "also designed, cut and sewed their own sails," ultimately going into business as sail-makers.

David Miller went on to cut his own wake as a winning racer, with the B.L. Johnson Trophy in 1957 and many more club trophies. His racing career has included the Sears Cup (emblematic of the North American Junior Championship, sailing with Colin Park, Ken Baxter and Bob Lance in Green Lake, Wisconsin), the Swiftsure, the North American Dragon Championships, the Albacore North American with Steve Tupper, and three Olympic Games in 1964, '68 and '72. In 1972, he brought home the RVYC's first Olympic medal in forty years, a bronze that he and team members Paul Cote, Jr., and John Ekels won in the Soling Class.

Like so many other families in the club, the Millers demonstrate the multigenerational membership of the club—and seeming proof that a love of the sea does run in the blood.

1972 Olympic sailing bronze medal winners (*left to right*) John Ekels, Dave Miller and Paul Cote, Jr.
Courtesy of Dave Miller

The Macnamara's Bowl team on the front lawn of the clubhouse in 1980, after winning the prize—a first for Canada. *Left to right:* Barbara Hartney, Cathy McPherson, Freydis Welland (who replaced Judy Day), Holly Everett, Lynne Newton and Sue Liebert.
Courtesy of Lynne Newton

had been an integral part of the decision-making process which ended with our present pristine site."

Solings arrived at the club in 1969 and within a year had grown into a fleet of nine boats. In 1972, Dave Miller took a new Soling, sponsored by fellow club member Bob Brodie, to the Olympics, where Miller and his crew of Paul Cote, Jr., and John Ekels won the bronze. The fleet at home expanded to fourteen boats, but by the late 1970s and early 1980s, the numbers subsided. Jack Balmer, an active Soling racer and coach for Canada's Olympic Soling team, noted that the club gained seventeen Solings in little more than a decade and that in that time they had twenty-six different names and "no less than forty-three owners. In retrospect, the Soling taught us all a lot about sailing, it brought an Olympic medal to the club, and it was great fun while it lasted."

Other classes that gained prominence in the 1970s and '80s included the Martin 242 (M242), which arrived in 1981. This high-performance racer-cruiser, designed and built by Donald Martin, became instantly popular, with sales to other parts of the world, and is now the largest one-design fleet at the RVYC.

The last three decades of the twentieth century were exciting years for the club, as it changed from what critics termed "exclusive" to more inclusive. Women gained a full vote in 1978, when the membership category of associate lady was abolished, thanks to the Province of British Columbia's new Human Relations Act and Societies Act. For the first time, "a woman can be an active member of RVYC with full voting and moorage privileges if she is prepared to pay the fees required."

An active group of women sailors did more than vote. These sailors—Judy Day, Annabelle Martin, Barb Ito and Lynne Brown (now Newton) among them—competed in the B.C. Sailing Championships, the Canadian Sailing Championships and the United States Yacht Racing Union's Women's Championships. As Lynne Newton reminisces: "In 1979 the Royal Lymington Yacht Club invited me to bring a women's team to England to compete in the Macnamara's Bowl (World Women's Keelboat Championships, 32-foot Contessas) against the English teams (who I had sailed with in 1977) and the European teams. The RVYC really rallied behind us, with training help from Donald Martin, Dave Miller and Tim Maledy, who gave us his new

The RVYC's winning crew aboard *Ultimatum* after the 1981 Emily Carr Regatta. *Left to right:* Holly Everett, Sue Liebert, Lisa Carstensen, Barbara Robinson and Lynne Newton.

Vancouver Sun Photo by Colin Price

32-foot boat to train in for the year. The club also hosted fundraising events to help defray the costs. It was the first time Canada had sent a women's team to a big boat regatta, and we all worked really hard to prove we could justify their pride. The team consisted of myself, Holly Maledy (now Everett), Judy Day, Sue Liebert, Barbara Hartney and Cathy McPherson. We went and, lo and behold, we won. (It was not that easy, I have to admit.) The club was very proud and so were we. Shortly thereafter, with Barbara Robinson added

to the crew, we went on to win the Emily Carr Regatta held in English Bay. Sue Liebert also went on to organize a crew and her boat for the Vic-Maui Race, and she often skippered *Sanfire* in local races as well. All these people were very active sailors either on their own or with family boats."

In September 1980, sixty-seven female members voted to form the Women's Committee, with Annabelle Martin elected as its first president. The committee's constitution stressed that its purpose was to "foster friendships and to promote

THE CLUB'S ORDNANCE

The Royal Vancouver Yacht Club has a collection of cannon and the Commodore's Gun Crew of junior and intermediate members commanded by the honorary master gunner. The Commodore's Cannon, a new piece cast from an old pattern and presented as a gift by retiring Commodore Bob Brodie in 1979, roars out the signal at the Sunset Ceremonies, Remembrance Day and on special occasions, such as the seventy-fifth anniversary of the Royal Canadian Navy, which was celebrated in style at the club.

An older gun, a carronade, a smaller weapon dating back to the nineteenth century, was presented to the club in 1906 by member J.E. Macrae. It was used as the signal gun until the arrival of the Commodore's Cannon. Another one, a line-throwing Lyle gun used to set the lines employed in shipwreck rescues, is a highly polished brass piece that dates to 1905.

A gun that spends considerable time at the RVYC is a small cast-iron cannon mounted on a base and presented to the Seattle Yacht Club in 1977 as the Wilson Trophy for Seamanship. The ties between the two clubs were strengthened in 1960, when they began to exchange visits on the occasion of each other's Opening Day. At Seattle's Opening Day in 1977, the RVYC fleet, headed by Lyall Bell's *Four Bells,* won the trophy for ship's appearance, crew deployment and adherence to protocol—and promptly took the cannon home. Seattle continued to lose its trophy for many years thereafter, save one, as Lyall Bell and crew continued their winning streak.

In 1985, when the RVYC regained the Wilson Trophy, Seattle's members claimed that it couldn't be found. Rather than argue the issue, the RVYC contingent enjoyed the hospitality of their hosts, and, at midnight, as Seattle's weary members headed for home, Commodore Patrick Oswald innocently asked the caretaker at the Seattle clubhouse if he could have access to the basement as he had left his sailing clothes there. Under cover of darkness, a group of RVYC yachtsmen quickly followed Oswald in, not to find his clothes but to search for the Wilson Trophy. They found it in the boiler room. Loading the cannon in a wheelbarrow and covering it, they wheeled their prize out and onto a boat, and once again the Wilson Trophy made its annual journey to Vancouver— to be eventually returned for the fun to start all over again, of course.

The Commodore's Gun Crew, shown here headed by Paul Wagner, stands at attention by the Commodore's Cannon.

Mistral, sailed by Bob Burgess, was the winner at the World Dragon Championship in 1983. The boat is still in the club, now owned by Heinz Rautenberg.

participation by all women members." Since that time, they have hosted many social and educational events and raised funds to purchase items for the club as well.

Other milestones during the period included the renovation of the clubhouse, with $1.7 million in repairs after the fire marshal, health department, liquor board and the labour department "condemned" it. The clubhouse, "on the verge of being closed," instead, after its 1979 recommissioning, served as the setting for more than fifty new events that have become traditions and remain in place as the RVYC passes one hundred, such as Robbie Burns Night, A Taste of the Orient, the Valentine's Day Dinner Dance, Big Band Night, the Spring Luncheon and Fashion Show, Candlelight Dinners, Theme Night, the Seafood Extravaganza, Oktoberfest and the Commodore's Ball. During those years, activities in the Jericho clubhouse were co-ordinated and overseen not only by the members but by the staff, led by a new general manager, James Dudley, who for over a decade and a half was a driving force as the club expanded and improved. Activities outside the clubhouse's walls also increased dramatically, with

more events on the water: Dog Days cruises, the Pacific Challenge Series, windsurfing and the Pacific Northwest Women's Invitational Can-Am Regatta.

Dog Days, inaugurated in 1971 by Fleet Captain Joe Glass, was intended to encourage new members—many of them novices who had joined because of the exceptional new moorage facilities at Jericho—to venture beyond English Bay or Howe Sound. The cruises into the Gulf Islands not only expanded the horizons of novice sailors but also achieved success as a family event. "The records of Dog Days Cruise '84 would seem to indicate that it was kids, kids, kids," reported Adrian Thomson and Joyce MacCrostie. "Not the real ones, of the goat variety, but the younger people who showed their elders a thing or two." Similarly, the Hazy Daze Cruise for power boaters, started in 1971 with the same agenda as Dog Days, ranged from the Gulf Islands to Desolation Sound.

One form of competition, predicted log racing, which had begun in the 1920s, with each skipper predicting the time it would take his boat to "cover the distance at a fixed number of engine revolutions," continued to develop into a sophisticated set of rules that test piloting, navigation and

Harvey Davidson sailing his *Wingaway* off Race Passage, competing in a Swiftsure race sometime in the 1970s.

The club's Royal Patron, His Royal Highness The Duke of Edinburgh, visited the RVYC in 1983 and was hosted by Commodore James Heaney.

seamanship. Some of North America's finest predicted log racers have come from the ranks of the RVYC, like Tom J. Trapp, who, with his vessel *Smitty,* was a driving force for three decades. Predicted log racing remains the subject of intense competition both in the club and the International Power Boat Association.

In 1987, continuing the club's long tradition of summer regattas, the first annual WAVES Regatta was initiated, chaired by Lisa Carstensen and Mike Clements, and currently organized by Tim Slaney. The focus was on a short course race for dinghies, but larger boats have since been added. This event coincided with the resurgence in competitive junior sailing, and its popularity draws sailors from the Pacific Northwest.

Ever active, the club's members continued to race in international competition. For the 1983 America's Cup, a number of RVYC sailors participated in the Secret Cove Yacht Club's challenge with *Canada I.* Steve Tupper, a veteran of the club's 1974 challenge and the Olympics, served as coach and manager prior to the event, until, he notes, "They ran out of money." That same year, Bob Burgess won the World Dragon Class Sailing

Championship and brought the Royal Hellenic Trophy to the club in triumph. The highlight of the year, however, was a royal visit by HRH The Duke of Edinburgh, who had become the club's Royal Patron in 1976. Commodore James Heaney welcomed the Royal Patron to the Jericho clubhouse in 1983, when he re-presented the Duke of Edinburgh Trophy to the Dragon fleet. That royal visit followed an earlier one by Prince Andrew, who had enjoyed it and obviously told his father. One reason for the young prince's fine memories may have been the relaxed time he spent on Lyall Bell's *Four Bells.* Kay Bell later recalled that the young prince, on a lunch cruise, returned to the table for more of her macaroni casserole. "'Ah, soul food,' he said. He was 'tired of smoked salmon.'"

TOWARD THE SECOND CENTURY

In 1986, Vancouver hosted Expo '86, invited the world and, as a result, changed even more into a world-class destination city. The RVYC's main event for Expo '86 was to host the International Yacht Racing Union (IYRU, now the International Sailing Federation) World Women's Sailing

At the Vancouver Area Racing
Council Regatta in the spring
of 1982. In the foreground,
Flattery (ex-*Pachena II*) then
owned by Dal Brynelsen, is in
pursuit of *Pachena III*.

Championships, while members and their boats participated in various Expo-related ceremonies and events. In the aftermath of the world's fair, Vancouver blossomed and so did the club. The 1990s also were a time of greater RVYC involvement in the community, with events like the Easter Seals Regatta, raising funds to support the Easter Seals assistance programs for children. In 1990, its first year, the event raised $80,000; in 1997, it raised $320,000. Other programs—the RVYC Special Children's Cruise and, in 1999, the inauguration of the Boat for Hope, also for children—demonstrated that the club was truly part of the community.

Long-range planning in the late 1980s and '90s focussed on the concept of "an unbroken string of outstations reaching from the U.S. border to Desolation Sound," with a "showcase destination in Howe Sound." At the same time, the club also made plans for an "additional Home Port marina, an objective driven by the awareness that the club's tenure in Coal Harbour" had always been subject to the shifting winds of politics and by a "long waiting list for sheltered moorage." The club invested in its facilities again in the '90s, extensively renovating the clubhouse, adding an underground parking garage beneath Hastings Park after four years of negotiations, a process

The Boat for Hope is one of the RVYC's many charitable activities in the community.

commenced in 1987 by Commodore J. Alex Wood. He remembers it well: the public hearing was "the longest in Vancouver's history," though "a few years later, the record was exceeded." The club upgraded its floating infrastructure and added to and improved the offshore stations, at a time when the economy was faring poorly. But members gave their time and services to assist, including one occasion when Jack Wood and Alex Wood dived on the rock hazards at Tugboat Island, set blasting charges, and "put the rocks in orbit." It was all in a day's work for the two engineers, though Alex recalls, "There are some disadvantages to being an engineer by profession, a boat builder by choice and a mechanic as a hobby."

Throughout the difficult economic conditions of the 1990s, the spirit of camaraderie and the triumphs of RVYC sailors in various competitions buoyed the club. Ross Macdonald, who started in the Junior Training Program and became the club's top Star sailor, raced in the 1988 Olympic Games at Seoul, and then went on with teammate Eric Jespersen to win a bronze at the 1992 Olympics in Barcelona. That win spurred him on to another goal, the World Star Championships. Three times he tried and failed, but as he said in 1994, "I knew we had the skills and experience to beat the field. We just had to be patient."

That patience paid off in 1994, when Macdonald and Jespersen beat ninety-seven boats from sixty-three nations to win the six-race World Star Championships. For the first time, a Canadian crew had won the world championship in the world's top one-design class. Macdonald also won four Bacardi Cups and raced in the Whitbread Round the World Race (now known as the Volvo Round the World Race) in 1997–98. His achievements, by the end of 2002, also included participating in the 1996 Olympic Games in Atlanta and the 2000 Games in Sydney, making him and Dave Miller the club's top Olympians. In 2003, Macdonald was in training for his fifth Olympic Games in 2004.

Club members also thrilled to Dan Sinclair's 1995 win of the Transpac with an all-Canadian crew of Ross Macdonald, Ron Ogilvy, John Campbell, John Cassils, Peter Fargey, Vlad Kahle, Dr Kevin McMeel, Dr. Jack Pacey, John Robertson and Don

Wright, who dubbed themselves "the weekend warriors." Sailing in the 20-metre ultralight *Merlin*, they relied on "good strategy, conservative tactics and consistent boat speed" to beat "some of the hottest space-age offshore drag-racers" skippered by "some of the most highly regarded names in professional yacht racing." The first Canadians to win a race that itself is nearly a century old, and most prestigious, Sinclair and his crew worked hard in an exceptional display of teamwork and won a place in international ocean-racing history. In 2001, Sinclair, in his 70-foot ultralight displacement boat *Renegade,* was still making headlines for his love of the sport and personal style.

Ross Macdonald with the trophy from his 1987 third place finish in the World Star Championships at Chicago. He is a racer whose competitions have brought fame and credit to the RVYC.
Jane Crawley photo, courtesy of the Macdonald family

Another member who added to the pride of the club in the 1990s and into the new millennium is Tine Moberg-Parker from Norway. After settling in Vancouver in 1988, where she met her husband, Dave Parker, at Simon Fraser University, Moberg-Parker's love of sailing manifested itself not only in competing at the club but also in serving as the head coach for the Junior Training Program. In 1991 she was world champion in the single-masted, 15-foot Europe Class competition and United States Yacht Racing Union's Woman Sailor of the Year in 1990 and '91. In 1993, Moberg-Parker decided to become a Canadian citizen and compete for Canada. By 1994, she had established herself as Canada's top woman dinghy sailor and as an inspiration at the club. A 1994 article in *Boat World* summed up her rapid rise to success: "When she joined the [Junior] Program in 1991 the racing team consisted of six sailors, and today there are 67 sailors from age 8 to 25, and the team has produced several

national champions." Moberg-Parker's success continued through the next decade, and she joined Ross Macdonald and other club sailors in reinforcing the Royal Vancouver Yacht Club's international reputation for excellence.

The notable success of the Junior Training Program, with a history that spans half of the RVYC's life, has been matched by the club's involvement in disabled sailing and the Paralympics. At the 2000 Olympic Games in Sydney, David Williams won the bronze in Sonar racing with teammates Brian MacDonald, "a 220-pounder with no legs below mid thigh," who had met Williams at the Mobility Cup when David was fleet captain, and Paul Tingley, who replaced earlier crew member Jamie Whitman, who, while an exceptional racer, made way for Tingley, who "was much stronger, taller (6′5″) and heavier than Jamie," explains Williams. After winning the competition to determine who would represent Canada on the

The Jericho mooring basin now hosts a large fleet, a major change from this location's 1920s origins as an exposed anchorage.

Olympic/Paralympic team, the crew worked hard. As David Williams explains, "You live and breathe the program. More paperwork, nutritionists, mental trainers, sailing till you're sick of it (well, not really!), going to the gym (I worked it out at lifting 46,000 pounds a week) and the constant search for money. I called in every favour I had out there to get coaching and dollars."

The Paralympics team was coached by the RVYC's Past Commodore Don Martin, who, in addition to being an international judge, boat designer, builder and rigger, was "a good friend and hard taskmaster" who also happened to be vice president of Canada's Olympic Development Committee. After shipping their new Sonar from Vancouver to Sydney, the team competed in what Williams says was "the most difficult place to sail I've ever encountered! It's extremely shifty and the variance in wind speed means constant gear shifts, every minute and a half or so. On top of that are what the locals call 'dark-

ies'; gust cells that come from the gradient above that hit with a 25- to 35-knot vertical gust. If you're in the right place at the right time, you'll be god; if not, dog meat." The final race had the Vancouver team in third place, with the bronze medal assured, behind the Germans in second place and the Australians in first. The Canadians tried to beat the Germans and grab the silver, but, despite their valiant try, the Germans sailed well and stayed in second place. For David Williams, it was "a real thrill to get an Olympic medal draped around my neck and I know my teammates felt the same. We were very proud to have represented Canada as well as we could and were proud to be Canadians."

A "storm of the century" in late December 2001 hit the club hard, causing some $500,000 in damage to the breakwater, floats and boats, as wind-driven waves battered English Bay. A measure of the club's strength—both in its leadership and its finances—was the speed with which it made repairs

The Junior Training Program remains an important and popular part of the RVYC's activities as the club begins its second century.

and absorbed the costs beyond what was insured. In that way, the RVYC is not just a club, an institution or a business—it is like a well-run ship, with a well-found captain and crew who have withstood the tests of time and storms of all sorts, both ashore and afloat. With its strong ties to the sea and to its shore community, the Royal Vancouver Yacht Club is a family of families, proud and ready to face the seas of the twenty-first century and beyond.

To KICK OFF its centennial year, the RVYC hosted a gala ball on 5 February 2003, with members attending in period costume, to commemorate its founding on that same day back in 1903. Past Commodore Patrick Oswald eloquently toasted the club with a review of its history and its sense of family, and was joined by other living past commodores in a salute to the RVYC. The centennial festivities continued in fine form with another Royal visit. On 8 May, HRH Prince Andrew took time during a busy visit to Vancouver to rededicate the club's Star & Dragon (formerly the Ports of Call) family dining area and pub, which featured a new addition—a junior's room, an area just for the juniors that highlights the RVYC's ongoing commitment to its youngest members. The prince—who is commodore of the Royal Thames Yacht Club and an avid sailor like his father, the club's Royal Patron—enjoyed his time at the club, mingling and talking with members. As he came to the club before another event—hence in black tie—Prince Andrew had his private secretary write that the visit while "necessarily brief and in the 'wrong rig' [was] a great pleasure." He also raised an amused eyebrow at the ornate uniform of the visiting admiral from the Seattle Yacht Club, who took the royal ribbing that followed with good humour.

The Opening Day Sail Past—the club's major centennial event—proved to be the largest in its history. With more than three hundred boats participating and more than eleven hundred members in attendance, the Sail Past and the Commodore's Reception that followed were also the longest in the club's history. Commodore John Dew probably shook more hands on a single occasion than any other commodore in the club's history and, certainly, standing on the deck of his flagship *Jess*, he

The RVYC's David Williams (skipper *top left*), Brian MacDonald (*bottom right*)and Paul Tingley (*bottom centre*) won a bronze medal at the Sydney Paralympics in 2000. Donald Martin (*top right*) coached the team and Jamie Whitman (*bottom left*) was the alternate.

STEVE TUPPER: CYA'S SAILOR OF THE YEAR FOR 2002

In 2002, the Canadian Yachting Association (CYA) presented its most prestigious award, Sailor of the Year, to Stephen Tupper. Active both within the Royal Vancouver Yacht Club and internationally, Tupper won his first trophy at age nine. In addition to serving as the first sailing instructor in the Junior Training Program in the 1950s, his work with the club has included an active role in committees supporting its elite sailors. While the CYA's award is an annual one, the recognition of Tupper was also made to honour his lifetime commitment to the sport of sailing. The award recognized that Tupper "has demonstrated sportsmanship, gained the respect of fellow sailors and provided recognition to the sport of sailing in Canada." The citation for the award summarizes the highlights of a sailor who has made his mark both on and off the water:

STEPHEN TUPPER has successfully represented Canada in the top echelons of international sailing. As an athlete, he finished 4th in Olympic competition (Dragon Class), won gold at numerous North American one-design championships, and sailed for Canada in many prestigious regattas such as the Admiral's Cup, Kenwood Cup, and Sardinia Cup. Stephen was a successful Team Leader and Coach for sailing in three Olympics and two Pan American Games, a coach and organizer of Canada's national teams, an International Jury member in three Olympics and a member of the jury of the Volvo Ocean Race and numerous world championships, a builder through his active involvement in the International Sailing Federation (ISAF) as a member of the ISAF and its various committees including events and race officials. There is no doubt that Stephen Tupper has been and will certainly continue to be a key influence and contributor for sailing in Canada and internationally.

OPENING DAY

The Royal Vancouver Yacht Club has many traditions and protocols that link the club of today not only with its earliest days but with the history of yachting and naval tradition. The protocol officer, appointed by the commodore, oversees these traditions: proper uniform and attire; etiquette in the clubhouse and afloat; rank, emblems and flags; visiting protocols and ceremonies. The longest serving protocol officer in the history of the club is Honorary Life Member Peter Veuger, who remained in office for thirty years until he retired in 2003.

Of all the traditions, the Opening Day Sail Past is the proudest event, and perhaps the most demonstrative, of the club's traditions. Its purpose is to pay respects to the commodore and is "an outward sign of an inner feeling" to honour members who serve and, therefore, contribute to the success of the club. The annual Sail Past in early May provides an opportunity for members to assemble, formally kitted out in dress uniform, to parade, in order, power and sail, from the largest yachts to the smallest dinghies, to exchange salutes with the commodore's flagship before dressing ship and anchoring. Once the Sail Past is completed, guests and crews retire to the clubhouse for a formal reception that culminates in the final drill for the stirring Sunset Ceremony of the lowering of Ensigns, accompanied by a military band and honour guard, and the firing of the evening gun by the Commodore's Gun Crew.

The Sail Past goes back to the earliest years of the club, with the first recorded one, a Flag Ceremony, held on 24 May 1935, as twenty-one powerboats and an unstated number of sailing craft turned out to salute Commodore Eric W. Hamber. Another Sail Past, in 1955, recorded 125 powerboats and an uncounted number of sailboats. The 1962 Sail Past was held on 12 May to honour Commodore Temp Wright. Since then, the Sail Past, with printed orders of the day, and in true spit-and-polish nature, has proceeded to honour the past and the present, sometimes in challenging circumstances, as the Opening Day notes for 1994 attest: "Needless to say this is sometimes a demanding task for all concerned, especially if there's a sharp blow."

The centennial Sail Past of May 2003 culminated in the traditional Sunset Ceremony. The flag officers salute the honour guard of Canadian Forces.

His Royal Highness Prince Andrew visited the club during the centennial celebrations in May 2003. After cutting the ribbon to inaugurate the newly opened Star & Dragon, he chatted informally with members. Here, he engages a member in conversation as Commodore John Dew looks on.
D.B. Sutcliffe photo

saluted more vessels in a single Sail Past than any previous commodore, a tangible reminder of how much the club has grown in the past hundred years.

Looking forward into the next century, the Royal Vancouver Yacht Club is in a superior financial condition, with assets reaching nearly $60 million in value. More than a social organization, with its assets the club is in many ways a substantial business operated on a not-for-profit basis for the benefit of its members. Governance of the club and its assets has, throughout its life, been critical, but has assumed even greater significance in the last decades. The club has been fortunate in its governance, as the executives of each year have worked to groom a succession of new leaders. As Bill Botham explains, "Having been caught up in and a member of the club for so many years, it was almost to be expected that I would become involved in the organization of the club. It starts out in volunteering to be on committees, and before you know you're on the executive of the club, and for some of us the path to becoming the commodore is inevitable, so we just sit back and enjoy it."

The Royal Vancouver Yacht Club, at the venerable age of one hundred, is one of Canada's and the world's great yacht clubs. As member Jim Burns points out, "In recent years, this club, along with the Royal Canadian Yacht Club in Toronto, has become known for producing the most talented sailors in the country. Our advantage—we can sail year round." As well, with its offshore stations and moorage facilities, the club is a major centre for power boating on the coast—an ideal springboard for its members to explore the rugged beauty and the isolation of the islands and fjords remain unchanged from the vistas that attracted recreational boaters a century ago. Hitting its stride at a hundred, the club remains strong: a 4400-member, 980-boat institution focussed on its family of members and the unique opportunities for racing and roving that first brought a group of yachtsmen together in 1903.

BIBLIOGRAPHY

BOOKS

Andersen, Doris. *The Columbia Is Coming!* Sidney, B.C.: Gray's Publishing Ltd., 1982.

Bell-Irving, Harry, and David D'Eath, Steven Grauer, John Hammond, Glen Hyatt, Robbie Rea, Dick Sandwell. *Offshore: Recollections of Gabrielle III, Racing and Cruising in the North and South Pacific, the North Atlantic and Scandinavian Waters, 1968–1971.* Vancouver: Dick Sandwell, 1993.

Carver, John Arthur. *The Vancouver Rowing Club: A History, 1886–1980.* Vancouver: Aubrey F. Roberts Ltd., 1980.

Cooper, William ("Vanderdecken"). *Yachts and Yachting; Being a Treatise on Building, Sparring, Canvassing, Sailing and the General Management of Yachts.* London: Hunt & Co., 1873.

Francis, Daniel, ed. *Encyclopedia of British Columbia.* Madeira Park, B.C.: Harbour Publishing, 2001.

Genders, Hilary, ed. *British Columbia Yachts: Building Dreams.* Vancouver: OP Publishing Ltd., 2002.

Gibson, Gordon, and Carol Renison. *Bull of the Woods: The Gordon Gibson Story.* Vancouver/Toronto: Douglas & McIntyre, 1980.

Golby, Humphrey, and Shirley Hewett. *Swiftsure: The First Fifty Years.* Sidney, B.C.: Lightship Press Limited, 1980.

Greene, Ruth. *Personality Ships of British Columbia.* West Vancouver, B.C.: Marine Tapestry Publications Ltd., 1969.

Hacking, Norman, and George A. Cran. *Annals of the Royal Vancouver Yacht Club, 1903–1970.* Third edition. Vancouver: Royal Vancouver Yacht Club, 1971.

Hacking, Norman. *The Two Barneys: A Nostalgic Memoir About Two Great British Columbia Seamen.* Vancouver: Gordon Soules Book Publishers Ltd., 1984.

Heaton, Peter. *A History of Yachting in Pictures.* London: Tom Stacey Ltd., 1972.

Henry, Tom. *Westcoasters: Boats That Built British Columbia.* Madeira Park, B.C.: Harbour Publishing, 1998.

Holm, Ed. *Yachting's Golden Age, 1880–1905.* New York: Alfred A. Knopf, 1999.

Hughes, John Scott. *Famous Yachts.* London: Methuen & Co., 1928.

MacCrostie, M. Watson, ed. *Annals of the Royal Vancouver Yacht Club, 1971–1985.* Vancouver: Royal Vancouver Yacht Club, 1986.

McCutchan, Philip. *Great Yachts.* London: Weidenfeld and Nicolson, 1979.

Macdonald, Bruce. *Vancouver: A Visual History.* Vancouver: Talonbooks, 1992.

McDonald, Robert A.J. *Making Vancouver: Class, Status and Social Boundaries, 1863–1913.* Vancouver: University of British Columbia Press, 1996.

McGowan, A.P. *Royal Yachts.* London: Her Majesty's Printing Office, 1977.

Mansbridge, Francis. *Launching History: The Saga of Burrard Dry Dock.* Madeira Park, B.C.: Harbour Publishing, 2002.

Matthews, Major J.S., *Early Vancouver.* Vols. 1 and 2. Vancouver: privately printed, 1932.

Morley, Alan. *Vancouver: From Milltown to Metropolis.* Vancouver: Mitchell Press, 1961.

Nicolls, Nan. *North of Anian, the Collected Journals of Gabrielle III: Cruises in British Columbia Coastal Waters, 1978–1989.* Vancouver: Dick Sandwell, 1990.

Nolan, Brian, and Brian Jeffrey Street. *Champagne Navy: Canada's Small Boat Raiders of the Second World War.* Toronto: Random House of Canada, 1991.

Oliver, Bet. *Ed Monk and the Tradition of Classic Boats.* Victoria: Horsdal & Schubart, 1998.

Reksten, Terry. *A Century of Sailing: A History of the Royal Victoria Yacht Club, 1892–1992.* Victoria: Orca, 1992.

Rousmaniere, John. *Fastnet, Force 10.* New York and London: W.W. Norton, 1980.

—. *The Luxury Yachts.* Alexandria, Va.: Time-Life Books, 1981.

Schreiner, John. *The Refiners: A Century of B.C. Sugar.* Vancouver/Toronto: Douglas & McIntyre, 1989.

Vassilopolous, Peter. *Antiques Afloat: From the Golden Age of Boating in British Columbia.* Vancouver: Panorama Publications, 1980.

Watts, Peter, and Tracy Marsh. *W. Watts & Sons, Boat Builders: Canadian Designs for Work and Pleasure, 1842–1946.* Oshawa, Ontario: Mackinaw Productions, 1997.

Whipple, A.B.C. *The Racing Yachts.* Alexandria, Va.: Time-Life Books, 1980.

Wynn, Graeme, and Timothy Oke. *Vancouver and Its Region.* Vancouver: University of British Columbia Press, 1992.

Articles

"About the Royal Vancouver Yacht Club–A Story of Ships." *Pacific Travel Monthly,* August 1936.

Hewett, Shirley. "The Prolific Henry Hoffar." *Pacific Yachting,* February 1998, 28-32.

Jensen, Vickie. "Rumrunner Update." *The Westcoast Mariner,* August 1988, 29-30.

"Motor Boating in Canada." *The Motor Boat,* 25 April 1906, 1-9.

Rogers, M.R. "*Mow Ping* and *Aquilo.*" *Pacific Yachting,* April 1999, 22-25.

Underwood, Jacqui. "The Romance of the Sea: History, Traditions, and the Legacy of the Royal Vancouver Yacht Club." *Vancouver Lifestyles,* Summer 2001, 22-25.

Periodicals

The Motor Boat
Pacific Yachting
Sea Breeze (the Royal Vancouver Yacht Club's newsletter, published first as *Motor Exhausts, Sailing Breezes* (1923-1927, then as *R.V.Y.C.* in 1935), then as *Sea Breeze*

from 1951 to the present)
Westcoast Mariner

Newspapers

Seattle Star
Seattle Times
Vancouver Daily Ledger
Vancouver Daily Province
Vancouver Province
Vancouver Sun
Vancouver World
Victoria Colonist
Victoria Times
Victoria Times-Colonist

Manuscripts

Cran, George A. "A Short History of the Royal Vancouver Yacht Club." Typescript, November 1957. Royal Vancouver Yacht Club Archives.

—. "Historical Records, Royal Vancouver Yacht Club, 1903-1931." Typescript, 1931. Royal Vancouver Yacht Club Archives.

Graveley, Walter E. "Recollections of a Long Life" [circa 1932]. Add. Mss. 147. Vancouver City Archives.

Letter book, 1909-1914, Royal Vancouver Yacht Club. Royal Vancouver Yacht Club Archives.

Moseley, Oswald. Scrapbook 1902-1956. Royal Vancouver Yacht Club Archives.

Sailing Committee Minutes, 1929-1941, Royal Vancouver Yacht Club. Royal Vancouver Yacht Club Archives.

Yacht *Vencedor,* logbook, 1931-1941. W.B. and M.H. Chung Library, Vancouver Maritime Museum.

INDEX

Peter Krivel-Zacks · Mary Kruger · Dan Kuhn · Stephen Leslie Kukucha · William Kunzweiler · Steven Kurrein · George Kurti · John D. Kyle · Dominique Labrosse

Thomas E. Ladner · Allan D. Laird · Franz Lajcik · Lindsay Lal · David C. Lam · Craig H. Lamb · Leslie Landes · Michael A. Lando · Ashley Lang · Margot Everett Lang · Rick Langer

Philip J. Langridge · Jean-Pierre Lapointe · Philip C. Lau · Cathryn J. Lawrence · Charles Lawson · David B. Lawson · Rebekah Lawson · Doug Le Patourel · Clement S.C. Lear

Catherine Leckie · Michael I. Leckie · Bruce W. Ledingham · Graham Lee · James Lee · Kent H. Lee · Robert Lee · Barbara Leech · Peter J. Leech · Allan James Lees

Henry Lees-Buckley · Barry V. Lehn · Brian Lehn · Arne Lehn · Martha Leigh · Murray J. Leith · Nicholas R. LeMoine · Tim Lepard · Jack Leshgold · Cameron P. Leslie · Pat Leslie

Richard K. Lester · W. Gordon Levett · Christopher Levy · Richard A. Lewall · Blakeney Lewis · Geoffrey Lewis · Herbert M. Lewis · Jack Leyland · John W. Leyland · Alden Li

Eric C.L. Li · Julie Lichtwer · Robert Liebert · Susan Mary Liebert · Fred Liebich · Thomas Lightburn · Ralph K. Lightheart Christopher A. Lilly · Sven Lincke · Richard Lindeman

Tanya Louise Listwin · Douglas John Little · James Doug Little · Jonathan Little · Phillip George Little · David E. Livingston · David N. Lloyd · Mark Lloyd · Patricia Lloyd

Marion Lochhead · Phillip Lockwood · Darlene Loftus-Buck · Bruce F. Long · John H. Long · Stuart A. Longair · J.D. Longley · Michael Lonsdale · Erik M. Loptson · Mark A.H. Loptson

Doreen Lougheed · Howard Louie · Paul Louie · Janice Low · Stephanie Lowe · Ralph W.P. Lowle · Paul J. Lowry · Peter D. Lowry · Stephen Lowry · Karen Lubin · Irene Lucas

Harald H. Ludwig · Russell R. Lumsden · Gar Lunney · Shane Lunny · Andrew Lyall · David Lyall · Teddi Lynn O. Lyall · John D. McAlduff · Jack McAllister · John McAllister

Ward McAllister · Rod H. McCallum · Henry A McCandless · Norman McCarvill · Doug McClary · Ralph McClellan · Janet McClelland · Bev McComb · Peter McComb

Richard McConnachie · John J. McCormack · John W. McCorquodale · Lori Patricia McCrady · Dale MacCrostie · Joyce MacCrostie-Shives · Richard MacCuish · Ross Allan McCutcheon

John C. McDermid · Mary McDermid · Scott McDermid · Adam Bruce Macdonald · Andrew MacDonald · Bree MacDonald · Brian MacDonald · Bruce MacDonald

David A.V. Macdonald · David F. MacDonald · D. Bruce Macdonald · D. Grant MacDonald · Glen McDonald · Ian Macdonald · James A. McDonald · Kenneth O. McDonald

Nancy M. Macdonald · Neil T. MacDonald · Ross Macdonald · Scott Macdonald · Tracy McDonald · William E. MacDonald · Patrick MacDougall · Catherine MacEachern

Donald F.J. McEachern · William Douglas McEachnie · Geoff McEvoy · Frank McFadden · Andrew McFarlane · John Macfarlane · Kim I. McFarlane · Robert G. McFarlane

Michael McGaw · Brenda McGill · Douglas Gordon McGillivray · Robert B. MacGillivray · Chris McGregor · James W. McGregor · M. Rob R. McGregor · Robert J. McGregor

Travis A. McGregor · Lee McGuire · Edward McIlwaine · Donald McInnes · Alexandra McIntyre · John Anthony McIntyre · Sheri-Lynn MacIntyre · Andrew Ewan MacKay

Andrew S. MacKay · George M. McKay · Harold L. MacKay · Iain Mackay · Joe McKay · Michael M. McKay · Robert M. Mackay · Margaret Mackay-Dunn · Clarke S. McKeen

G. Craig McKeen · Graeme McKenney · Donald Fraser McKenzie James MacKenzie · Ronald M. MacKenzie · Stephen MacKenzie · Guy McKenzie-Smith · Michael McKone

George P. McLauchlin · Kathryn McLaughlin · Alan MacLean · Brennen McLean · Cameron J. McLean · David G. McLean · David I. McLean · Elizabeth McLean · Ian A. MacLean

Jason McLean · Kenneth E. McLean · Kim McLean · Sacha McLean · Victor F. MacLean · James Duncan McLennan · Mark J. McLennan · Michael John McLennan

N. Hume McLennan · Donald MacLeod · Jonathan Campbell McNair · Charles J. McNeely Jr. · Thomas McNeely · Dawn Ellen McNevin · Hugh C. MacNiel · James A. McPhail

Terry J. McPhail · James C. McPhalen · Cathy McPherson · Douglas C. McPherson · Duncan McPherson · Ian McPherson · James McPherson · Jillian MacPherson

John G. Macpherson · Christine McPhie · Norman J. McQuade · Mark McQuillen · Bernice McRae · Eunice McRae · Kenneth I. McRae · Ralph McRae · James McRoberts

Robert M. MacWhirter · Alan K. Mackworth · Michael F. Madsen · George Magnus · Christy Mahoney · John A. Mahoney · Klaus Mai · Kenneth J. Mair · Rafe Mair · Robert G. Mair

Ian D. Maitland · Jeanie E. Maitland · Stephen F. Majoros · Randall C. Malcher · Claudia Maledy · Timothy Maledy · Eleanor Malkin · H. Louise Malkin · Patrick William Maloney

Loretto Mann · Gerrard Eric Manning · Glen T. Manning · Juanita Manning · Michael G. Manning · Stuart A. Manning · Velma Mansell · Gillian J. Manson · Robin J. Manson

Ronald L. Marcoux · Glen R. Mardon · Linda Mari · Nicholas G. Marinatos · Maike Marnet · Barry Marsden · Harry J. Marshall · Annabelle J. Martin · Brent R. Martin

Christopher Martin · Donald A. Martin · Jennifer J. Martin · Marylile Martin · Shane Martin · Teesa Martin · John Martyn · R. Bruce Martyn · Philip S. Marx · David J. Mason

Donald R. Mason · J. George Mason · John H.M. Mason · Sandra Mason · Douglas J. Mass · Gene J. Mass · George William Matheson · Ryan A. Matheson · William J. Mathisen

Bob V. Matthews · Bruce A. Matthews · Brian J. Maunder · Marleen Mavrow · R.H. Mark Mawhinney · John Maxon · James Ian Maxwell-Smith · William May

James R. Maze · Dennis A. Meakin · Gladys Meakin · Howard D. Meakin · Jean Meakin · Grant Mebs · Grant P. Meeres · Michael Keith Meinhardt · Christie Meldrum

Kennith A. Mellquist · Adrienne Elizabeth Mennell · Herbert J. Menten · James Mercier · Scott Meredith · Thomas Merinsky · James H. Merritt · Stuart R. Messenger

L.H. Michalson · Carsten Mide · W.R. Miles · Arnold Miles-Pickup · Brad Miller · David S. Miller · Gilmore E. Miller · Ronald G. Miller · Michael Mills · Vera Milne Kilcoyne

D.F. (Ted) Milner · Gary Minielly · Barry Mitchell · Gordon Mitchell · Keith E.W. Mitchell · Tine Moberg-Parker · Carey Mobius · Peter Moes · Rowena Moffett

Russell Moldowan · Andre A. Molnar · Dak Molnar · Anneliese Monk · Ronald John Monk · Ronald D. Moody · Arthur Donald Moore · Catherine E. Moore · M.H. Moore

Peter S. Moore · Ronda Lynn Moore · Troy Moreira · Don Morgan · John Morgan · John F. Morgan · C.E. Morris · Jeffrey Morris · Samantha Morris · David D. Morrison

Robert T. Morrison · Alan G. Morse · Anne Morse · Colin Morse · Jonathan A. Morse · Kean Morse · Margaret Mortifee · Anita Morton · Douglas Moseley · Robert Moseley

Gary Muchula · Gerd Mueller · Ian Munro · Craig Munroe · David Murphy · H. Ormond Murphy · Robert M. Murphy · Angus Murray · Donald E. Murray

Wm. Trevor Murrie · Brian Naphtali · Alison H. Narod · Eileen-Louise Narod · Jeffrey A. Narod · Hugh Nash · Andreas Naumann · Brent G. Naylor · Craig Naylor

Wayne T. Naylor · Omar Nazif · Miroslav Neckar · Rae J. Nelson · Richard I. Nelson · Patrick Nevison · James Gilmour Newall · Stephen Newell · Barbara Newton

John F. Newton · Lynne R. Newton · Trevor M. Newton · D. Maureen Neylan · David Neylan · Margaret Neylan · Meghan S. Neylan · Shawn Craig D. Neylan · Richard S. Nicholls

Roderick P.R. Nicolls · Leanne Niewerth · Egon Nikolai · Troy Nikolai · Alexandra Noble · Bruce David Nolan · Caroline Marie North · Robert James North · Rory North

Rudy North · Robert Clifford Northcott · Florence Northrop · Gary F. Nott · Robert E. Nowack · Arnold Langley Nunn · Brian O'Connell · Edward Odishaw · Ron Ogilvy

Nicole A. Olafson · Randall A. Olafson · A. David F. Oland · Peter Wm. Falconer Oland · Glen Olds · Clifford Charles Oleksiew · Douglas K. Oliver · Janet Oliver

Michael S. Oliver · Oluf W. Olsen · John S. Olson · Mervyn D. Olson · Michael Olson · Dean Olund · Dexter G. Olund · Susan E. O'Reilly · Bruce Orr · Grace Orr · Richard R. Orr

Robert R. Orr · Tom F. Orr · R.A. Osborne · Brian J. O'Sullivan · A.J. Patrick Oswald · Hugh S.C. Oswald · Michael J.C. Oswald · Patrick W.T.C. Oswald · Beverley L. O'Toole

James D. Ott · Judith Ann Ouellette · Julia A.L. Oulton · Roger F. Ovens · Christian S. Owen · Katherine Owens · John Allan Pacey · Katrina Pacey · Michael Padwick

J. Michael Page · John G. Page · Justin Page · Rebecca Page · Lawrence Page · Milton G. Pahl · Georges Pahud · John Henry Painter · Dorina Palmer · Nicholas Andrew Palmer

Patrick M. Palmer · Ronald E. Pampu · Andy Papp · Robert Pappajohn · Cameron Park · Sandy Park · J. David Parker · L.F. Parker · Patricia Parker · Philip Parker

Robert Scott Parker · Ron Parker · John M. Parks · Shalan Parks-Jaye · David Parsons · Frank Parsons · Giles Parsons · Raymond L. Parsons · Vivian Parsons · Robert C. Parton

Tone Paterson · Lynn Patterson · James A. Pattison · Sarah R. Pattison · Ray Pauls · Robert G. Payne · Robert L. Payne · Dave Pearce · Dean K. Pearce · Duncan Pearce

Kenneth R.W. Pearce · Todd O. Pearce · John W. Pearson · Roger H. Pearson · Andrew Peck · Robert James Peck · Annie Pedersen · Gordon Pedersen · James M. Pedersen

Lars Pedersen · Paul Peek-Philpott · Cyndy Pellegrin · David R. Pendleton · John W. Perchall · Donald E. Percy · George E. Percy · Ronald John Percy · Alan R. Peretz

Dwight Gregg Peretz · Geoffrey D. G. Peretz · Michael T. Peter · John D. Peters · J.R. (Ray) Peters · Erik B. Peterson · Steven D. Pettigrew · David Phillips · Dean Phillips

Lorna Phillips · Dennison John Pickering · Walter Pilutik · Carl J. Pines · Sandy Pitfield · Vladimir Plavsic · Joel Podersky-Cannon · David Podmore · John Polglase · Philip Porter

Douglas Portfors · Ernest Andrew Portfors · David Pottinger · Russell Poulston · Hein Poulus · Ronald Pousette · Peter S. Powers · William Powers · Tammy Preast-Bolton

James S. Prentice · Edward Prescesky · Peter Preston · E.V. (Ted) Price · Marie Jose Price · Robert Bruce Pridmore · Jason B. Priestley · Lorne D. Priestley · E. Scott Primrose

T.R. Brian Pritchard · David Probyn · Edward R. Probyn · Jennifer Provan · Kerry L. Pruden · Marilyn Pruden · William A. Puckering · Keith Purchase · R.W. Purdie

Todd Dickson Hugh Purdie · Hamish Purdy · Irene Purdy · John Purdy · Robert Purdy · Erica Purves · Alan Pyatt · Leonard Pye · Matthew Quinlan · Douglas Race · William R. Race